Introduction to labour laws

Sujata Pawar

Copyright© Sujata Sanjay Pawar
ISBN-13: 978-1540497888
ISBN-10: 1540497887

Contents

Preface

1 Introduction to labour law in India   9

2 Constitution of India and labor laws   14

3 Registration of Trade Union   21

4 Rights of Registered Trade Unions   27

5 Workman's Compensation   33

6 Amount of Compensation   38

7 Payment of Wages   43

8 Authorized Deduction from Wages   48

9 Inspectors   55

Preface

The law relating to labour and employment occupies an important place in the regulation of industry and employment and hence they are also referred as Industrial laws. These laws regulate the employer-employee relationship and helps in the maintenance of industrial peace and harmony and prevent industrial unrest.

The growth and development of industry is vital for countries like India, which have abundant natural resources, population and potency to excel. The industrial growth in the domestic market pushes higher growth rate in terms of production and consumption. Thus the role of labour laws in the present scenario has become more important.

This book is an attempt to simplify labour legislation and I hope this book will assist law students, teachers, lawyers and laymen equally. If the book proves to be of the slightest use to those for whom it has been written, I shall feel my labor amply rewarded. The constructive suggestions from the readers will always be welcome.

I would like to express my gratitude to all those who have guided and helped me in the accomplishment of this task. First of all I owe my gratitude to my research guide, Dr. D. S Ukey, Ex Vice Chancellor, SRTM University, Nanded, and Head, Department of law, University of Pune, for providing me his valuable guidance. I am indebted to my mentors Adv. K. V. Patil, Adv. D. V. Patil and Adv. D I S Mulla for their kind guidance and valuable suggestions. I also owe my gratitude to Dr. N. D. Patil, Dr. Anil Patil, Prin. Dr Ganesh Thakur and Prin. Dr. D. D. Patil from Rayat Shikshan Sanstha, for their constant encouragement and support in this endeavor.

The publisher deserves compliments for bringing out this book so neatly, expeditiously and in an attractive manner. I take this opportunity to convey my feelings of gratitude to my colleague Prof. Yogesh Kolekar, for his scholarly efforts. I extend my sincere thanks to them and all my friends and colleagues who helped me and encouraged me in bringing out this work.

Dr. Sujata Pawar

Chapter 1

Introduction to labour law in India

The labour laws are laws, rules and regulation related to employment and also known as employment law. These laws regulate the working of employees,[1] provides registration of trade unions,[2] establishes Labour Courts,[3] provides for minimum wages[4] etc.

These laws regulate the relationship between employer and employee aiming for a healthy working environment and protection of worker form exploitations.

It is aptly said that labour law is the child of the industrial revolution, thus in India the formal traces of labour laws goes back to the pre independence era where in the year the Factory Act, 1881 was enacted to improve the working conditions workers and children in factories.[5]

---

[1] Regulates working hours, provides for safe working environment etc.
[2] The Trade Union Act, 1926
[3] Established under provisions of Industrial Disputes Act 1947
[4] The Minimum Wages Act, 1948
[5] http://holisticthought.com/india-under-the-british-lord-ripon/

The Workmen's Compensation Act, 1923 provides for payment of compensation in case of injury or death. Further in the year 1926 a milestone was created with the enactment of the Trade Union Act, 1926 which gave legal recognition to trade unions in India thereby leading to regulated growth in the industrial sphere.

The post independence saw a tremendous growth in the industrial activity which was supported by the legal regime of labour laws and important enactment like the Trade Dispute Act, 1947 which provided a machinery for dispute resolution and provided the procedures for strike and lockout. Further the Employees' State Insurance Act, 1948 laid the welfare scheme for the worker in case injury, sickness, maternity, disablement, death etc.

The following are the essential legislation under the labour laws,

1) The Fatal Accidents Act,1855[6]

2) The Indian Boilers Act,1923[7]

3) The Trade Union Act, 1926[8]

4) The Workmen Compensation Act, 1923[9]

---

[6] http://indiacode.nic.in/rspaging.asp?tfnm=185513
[7] http://www.theindianlawyer.in/statutesnbareacts/acts/i11.html
[8] http://www.ilo.org/dyn/natlex/docs/WEBTEXT/32075/64876/E26IND01.htm
[9] http://indiacode.nic.in/fullact1.asp?tfnm=192308

5) The Payment Of Wages Act, 1936[10]

6) Industrial Employment and Standing Orders Act,1946[11]

7) The Industrial Disputes Act, 1947[12]

8) The Minimum Wages Act, 1948[13]

9) The Employees State Insurance Act, 1948[14]

10) The Factories Act, 1948[15]

11) The Plantations Labour Act,1951[16]

12) The Mines Act,1952[17]

13) The Employee Provident Fund And Miscellaneous Provision Act, 1952[18]

---

[10] http://www.ilo.org/dyn/travail/docs/625/Payment%20of%20Wages%20Act%201936.pdf
[11] http://www.vakilno1.com/bareacts/industrialemploymentact/industrialemploymentact.htm
[12] https://indiankanoon.org/doc/500379/
[13] http://www.ilo.org/dyn/travail/docs/623/Minimum%20Wages%20Act%201948.pdf
[14] http://www.esic.nic.in/Tender/ESIAct1948Amendedupto010610.pdf
[15] https://www.ilo.org/dyn/natlex/docs/WEBTEXT/32063/64873/E87IND01.htm
[16] http://www.labour.nic.in/sites/default/files/ThePlantationLabourAct1951.pdf
[17] http://indiacode.nic.in/fullact1.asp?tfnm=195235
[18] http://www.epfindia.com/site_docs/PDFs/Downloads_PDFs/EPFAct1952.pdf

14) The Maternity Benefits Act, 1961[19]

15) The Apprentices Act, 1961[20]

16) The Payment Of Bonus Act, 1965[21]

17) The Contract Labour (Regulation And Abolition) Act, 1970[22]

18) The Payment Of Gratuity Act, 1972[23]

19) The Equal Remuneration Act, 1976[24]

20) The Dangerous Machines (Regulation) Act, 1983[25]

21) The Child Labour (Prohibition and Regulation) Act, 1986[26]

22) The Building and Other Construction Workers (Regulation of Employment and working Conditions) Act, 1996[27]

---

[19] http://www.ilo.org/dyn/travail/docs/678/maternitybenefitsact1961.pdf
[20] http://www.dget.nic.in/content/innerpage/apprentices-act-1961.php
[21] http://labour.bih.nic.in/acts/payment_of_bonus_act_1965.pdf
[22] http://labour.bih.nic.in/Acts/contract_labour_regulation_and_abolition_act_1970.pdf
[23] http://www.labour.nic.in/sites/default/files/ThePaymentofGratuityAct1972.pdf
[24] http://labour.gov.in/sites/default/files/equal_remuneration_act_1976_1.pdf
[25] http://www.vakilno1.com/bareacts/dangeriousmachinesact/dangerousmachinesact.htm
[26] http://labour.gov.in/sites/default/files/act_3.pdf
[27] http://indiacode.nic.in/fullact1.asp?tfnm=199627

23) The Building and Other Construction Workers Welfare Cess Act, 1996[28]

24) Unorganized Workers Social Security Act, 2008[29]

25) Sexual Harassment of Women at Workplace (Prevention, Prohibition and Redressal) Act, 2013[30]

---

[28] http://hrylabour.gov.in/docs/labourActpdfdocs/Cess_Act.pdf
[29] http://labour.gov.in/sites/default/files/TheUnorganisedWoekersSocialSecurityAct2008_0.pdf

Chapter 2

Constitution of India and labor laws

The Constitution of India confers and uphold the rights of workers through fundamental rights and Directive Principles of State Policy. Article 14[31] of the Constitution of India provides equality before the law. This principle is enforced through the Equal Remuneration Act, 1976.

The object of the Equal Remuneration Act, 1976, is to provide equal remuneration for men and women for the same work and to prevent discrimination against women during recruitment.

The Act establishes Advisory committees for the promotion of employment opportunities for women. The object of the Act says,

---

[30] http://wcd.nic.in/act/sexual-harassment-women-workplace-preventionprohibition-and-redressal-act-2013

[31] Equality before law The State shall not deny to any person equality before the law or the equal protection of the laws within the territory of India Prohibition of discrimination on grounds of religion, race, caste, sex or place of birth

"Article 39 of Constitution envisages that the State shall direct its policy, among other things, towards securing that there is equal pay for equal work for both men and women.

To give effect to this constitutional provision, the President promulgated on the 26th. September, 1975, the Equal Remuneration Ordinance, 1975 so that the provisions of Article 39 of the Constitution may be implemented in the year which is being celebrated as the International Women's Year. The Ordinance provides for payment of equal remuneration to men and women workers for the same work or work of similar nature and for the prevention of discrimination on grounds of sex. (2) The Ordinance also ensures that there will be no discrimination against recruitment of women and provides for the setting up of Advisory committees to promote employment opportunities for women. The Bill seeks to replace the Ordinance."

The Article 19(1)(c)[32] of the Constitution is enforced through the Trade union act 1926. The Trade Union Act, 1926 provides for registration of trade unions in India and provides rights to registered trade unions. The Act in its object says,

"An Act to provide for the registration of Trade Unions and in certain respects to define the law relating to registered Trade Unions. "

---

[32] to form associations or unions

The Article 21[33] of the Constitution provides for the right to life. The Supreme Court had upheld that right to life means right to live with human dignity[34] including the right to livelihood.[35] The Article 23[36] of the Constitution prohibits trafficking in human beings and forced labor.

The Bonded Labour System System (Abolition) Act of 1976 prohibits beggar and other similar forms forced labour. The Act abolishes bonded labour system or any other form of forced labour.

The object of the Act says,

"There still exists in different parts of the country a system of usuary under which the debtor or his decendants or dependants have to work for the creditor without reasonable wages or with no wages in order to extinguish the debt. At times, several generations work under bondage for the repayment of a paltry sum which had been taken by some remote ancestor.

---

[33] Protection of life and personal liberty No person shall be deprived of his life or personal liberty except according to procedure established by law

[34] Francis Coralie Mullin v. Administrator, Union Territory of Delhi and others, 1981 AIR 746, 1981 SCR (2) 516

[35] D.K. Yadav vs J.M.A. Industries Ltd, 1993 SCR (3) 930, 1993 SCC (3) 259, Olga Tellis & Ors vs Bombay Municipal Corporation, 1986 AIR 180, 1985 SCR Supl. (2) 51, Peoples Union for Democratic Rights v. Union of India, 1982 AIR 1473, 1983 SCR (1) 456

[36] Prohibition of traffic in human beings and forced labour, (1) Traffic in human beings and begar and other similar forms of forced labour are prohibited and any contravention of this provision shall be an offence punishable in accordance with law.
(2) Nothing in this article shall prevent the State from imposing compulsory service for public purpose, and in imposing such service the State shall not make any discrimination on grounds only of religion, race, caste or class or any of them.

The interest rates are exorbitant and such bondage Can not be interpreted as the result of any legitimate contract or agreement. The system implies the infringement of the basic human rights and destruction of the dignity of human labour.

Article 23(1) of the Constitution prohibits "begar" and other similar forms of forced labour and further provides that any contravention of the said prohibition shall be an offence punishable in accordance with law ......"

The Supreme Court has held that Article 23 prohibits forced labour and declares it, a violation of human dignity and contrary to basic human values.[37]

Article 24[38] in the Constitution prohibits employment of children below 14 years of age in factory, mine or any other hazardous employment.

This provision of the constitution is implemented through the Child Labour (Prohibition and Regulation) Act, 1986 which prohibits child labour. The object of the Act is,

---

[37] People'S Union For Democratic .. vs Union Of India & Others, 1982 AIR 1473, 1983 SCR (1) 456, Sanjit Roy vs State Of. Rajasthan, 1983 AIR 328, 1983 SCR (2) 271

[38] Prohibition of employment of children in factories, etc No child below the age of fourteen years shall be employed to work in any factory or mine or engaged in any other hazardous employment Provided that nothing in this sub clause shall authorise the detention of any person beyond the maximum period prescribed by any law made by Parliament under sub clause (b) of clause (7); or such person is detained in accordance with the provisions of any law made by Parliament under sub clauses (a) and (b) of clause(7)

"An Act to prohibit the engagement of children in all occupations and to prohibit the engagement of adolescents in hazardous occupations and processes and the matters connected therewith or incidental thereto."

Directive Principles of State Policy[39]

The directive principles of state policy are directives to the state/Government to adopt these principles in practice through enactments.

The following are the directive principles of state policy related to labour laws and welfare.

1) Certain principles of policy to be followed by the State: The State shall, in particular, direct its policy towards securing

(a) that the citizens, men and women equally, have the right to an adequate means to livelihood;

(b) that the ownership and control of the material resources of the community are so distributed as best to subserve the common good;

---

[39] The provisions contained in this Part shall not be enforceable by any court, but the principles therein laid down are nevertheless fundamental in the governance of the country and it shall be the duty of the State to apply these principles in making laws.

(c) that the operation of the economic system does not result in the concentration of wealth and means of production to the common detriment;

(d) that there is equal pay for equal work for both men and women;

(e) that the health and strength of workers, men and women, and the tender age of children are not abused and that citizens are not forced by economic necessity to enter avocations unsuited to their age or strength;

(f) that children are given opportunities and facilities to develop in a healthy manner and in conditions of freedom and dignity and that childhood and youth are protected against exploitation and against moral and material abandonment.[40]

2) Right to work, to education and to public assistance in certain cases. The State shall, within the limits of its economic capacity and development, make effective provision for securing the right to work, to education and to public assistance in cases of unemployment, old age, sickness and disablement, and in other cases of undeserved want.[41]

---

[40] Article 39 in The Constitution Of India 1949
[41] Article 41 in The Constitution Of India 1949

3) Provision for just and humane conditions of work and maternity relief The State shall make provision for securing just and humane conditions of work and for maternity relief.[42]

4) Living wage, etc, for workers The State shall endeavor to secure, by suitable legislation or economic organisation or in any other way, to all workers, agricultural, industrial or otherwise, work, a living wage, conditions of work, ensuring a decent standard of life and full enjoyment of leisure and social and cultural opportunities and, in particular, the State shall endeavor to promote cottage industries on an individual or cooperative basis in rural areas.[43]

5) Participation of workers in management of industries The State shall take steps, by suitable legislation or in any other way, to secure the participation of workers in the management of undertakings, establishments or other organizations engaged in any industry.[44]

6) Duty of the State to raise the level of nutrition and the standard of living and to improve public health The State shall regard the raising of the level of nutrition and the standard of living of its people and the improvement of public health as among its primary duties and, in particular, the State shall endeavor to bring about prohibition of the consumption except for medicinal purposes of intoxicating drinks and of drugs which are injurious to health.[45]

---

[42] Article 42 in The Constitution Of India 1949
[43] Article 43 in The Constitution Of India 1949
[44] Article 43A in The Constitution Of India 1949
[45] Article 47 in The Constitution Of India 1949

Chapter 3

Registration of Trade Union

A trade union[46] in India is registered under the provisions of the Trade Union Act, 1926 and is applicable to the whole of India. A trade union is an organization formed primarily for the purpose of regulating the relationship between the following,

1) Workmen and employers

2) Workmen and workmen

3) Employers and employers

---

[46] Sec.2(h) of the Trade Union Act, 1926, "trade union" means any combination, whether temporary or permanent, formed primarily for the purpose of regulating the relations between workmen and employers or between workmen and workmen, or between employers and employers, or for imposing restrictive conditions on the conduct of any trade or business, and includes any federation of two or more trade unions.

It is established to promote the objects of the trade unions and includes any federation of two or more trade unions. The appropriate government[47] appoints Registrar[48] of each state.[49]

Mode of Registration

Any seven or more members of a trade union can apply for registration by giving an application along with a copy of rules to the Registrar with a statement on following,[50]

1) The names, occupations and addresses of the members making the application.

2) The name of the trade union and the address of its head office.

3) The titles, names, ages, addresses and occupations of the of the trade union.[51]

---

[47] Sec.2 of the Trade Union Act, 1926, the appropriate government" means, in relation to trade unions whose objects are not confined to one State, the Central Government, and in relation to other trade unions, the State Government, and], unless there is anything repugnant in the subject or context

[48] Sec.2(f) of the Trade Union Act, 1926, "Registrar" means- (i) a Registrar of Trade Unions appointed by the appropriate government under section 3, and includes any Additional or Deputy Registrar of Trade Unions, and (ii) in relation to any trade union, the Registrar appointed for the state in which the head or registered office, as the case may be, of the trade union is situated;]

[49] Sec.3 of the Trade Union Act, 1926

[50] Sec.4 of the Trade Union Act, 1926

[51] Sec.5 of the Trade Union Act, 1926

If a trade union is already in existence for more than a year, then such trade union shall also submit a general statement of the assets and liabilities of the trade union[52] along with the application to the registrar.[53]

Rules of a Trade Union

The copy of rules shall contain the following matters,

1) The name of trade union.

2) The objects for which the trade union has been established.

3) The purposes for which the general funds of the trade union shall be applicable.

4) The maintenance of a list of the members of the trade union and adequate facilities for the inspection by the office-bearers and members of the trade union.

5) The admission of ordinary members, honorary or temporary members as office bearers required to form the executive of the trade union.

---

[52] In a prescribed form
[53] Sec.5(1)(2) of the Trade Union Act, 1926

6) The payment of a subscription by members of the trade union.

7) The conditions under which any member shall be entitled for any benefit, fine or forfeiture which may be imposed on the members.

8) The process by which the rules shall be amended, varied or rescinded.

9) The mode by which the members of the executive, office-bearers of the trade union shall be appointed and removed.

10) The safe custody of the funds of the trade union and annual audit, and regarding adequate facilities for the inspection of the account books of the trade union.

11) The manner in which the trade union may be dissolved.

Registration

The Registrar shall register the trade union after compliance with requirements and shall register the trade union in the register maintained for such purpose.[54] The Registrar shall issue a certificate of registration upon registration, which shall be a conclusive evidence that the trade union is registered under the Trade Union Act, 1926.[55]

---

[54] Sec.8 of the Trade Union Act, 1926
[55] Sec.9 of the Trade Union Act, 1926

A registered trade union shall be a body corporate having perpetual succession, common seal, power to hold both movable and immovable property and can sue and be sued.[56]

Cancellation

A trade union can be cancelled by the Registrar on the following grounds,

1) On application of the trade union.[57]

2) If the trade union is registered by mistake.

3) If the registration is done by fraud.

4) If the trade union has ceased to exist.

5) If the trade union willfully continues to contravene the provisions of the trade unions Acts, 1926 and a notice in this regard has been issued by the Registrar.

---

[56] Sec.13 of the Trade Union Act, 1926
[57] Sec.10(a) of the Trade Union Act, 1926

A notice of not less than two months shall given specifying the reason for the cancellation of a trade union by the Registrar to the trade union. An appeal[58] against the decision of the Registrar for refusal to register a trade union and withdrawal or cancellation of a trade union can be preferred to the prescribed authority.[59]

---

[58] Sec.11 of the Trade Union Act, 1926

Chapter 4

Rights of Registered Trade Unions

Rights of a Registered Trade Unions[60]

To establish general fund and to spend funds on its object. A registered trade union shall not be spent funds on any other objects than the following,

(1) To make payment of salaries, allowances and expenses of office-bearers of the trade unions.

(2) To make payment for the expenses for the administration of the trade union, including audit.

---

[59] Any person aggrieved by any refusal of the Registrar to register a trade union or by the withdrawal or cancellation of a certificate of registration may, within such period as may be prescribed, appeal- (a) where the head office of the trade union is situated within the limits of a Presidency town to the High Court, or (b) where the head office is situated in any other area, to such Court, not inferior to the court of an additional or assistant Judge of a principal civil court of original jurisdiction, as the appropriate government may appoint in this behalf for that area……
[60] Sec.15 of the Trade Union Act, 1926

(3) For the prosecution or defense of any legal proceeding to which the trade union or any member thereof is a party.

(4) To conduct of trade disputes on behalf of the trade union or any member.

5) To provide compensation to the members for loss arising out of trade disputes.

6) To provide allowances to members or their dependents on account of death, old age, sickness, accidents or unemployment.

(7) The issue policies of assurance on the lives of members, or policies insuring members against sickness, accident or unemployment.

8) To make provisions of education, social or religious benefits for members or for the dependants of members.

(9) For the periodical published.

To establish a separate fund for political purposes[61]

A registered may establish a separate fund for the promotion of civic and political interest of its members[62] and for the furtherance of objects like the payment of any expenses incurred by a candidate or prospective candidate for election as a member of any legislative body,[63] for conduct of any meeting, distribution of any literature,[64] maintenance of any person who is the member of any legislative body constituted,[65] for the registration of electors or the selection of a candidate for any legislative body constituted,[66] the holding of political meetings.[67]

Criminal conspiracy in trade disputes

Section 17 of the Trade Union Act, 1926 provides immunity to the members and office bearer of a registered trade union from punishment under sub-section (2) of section 120B of the Indian Penal Code, 1860 for any agreement between the members of the trade union in the furtherance of any object of the trade union specified under the section 15.

---

[61] Sec.16 of the Trade Union Act, 1926
[62] Sec.16(1) of the Trade Union Act, 1926
[63] Sec.16(2)(a) of the Trade Union Act, 1926
[64] Sec.16(2)(b) of the Trade Union Act, 1926
[65] Sec.16(2)(c) of the Trade Union Act, 1926
[66] Sec.16(2)(d) of the Trade Union Act, 1926
[67] Sec.16(2)(e) of the Trade Union Act, 1926

However, this immunity shall not be applicable if such agreement is an agreement to commit any offense.

Immunity from civil suit[68]

A registered trade union[69] is provided with civil immunity from legal proceeding in respect of any act done in furtherance of a trade dispute to which a member of the trade union is a party on the ground only that such act induces any person to break a contract of employment, or interference with the trade, business or employment of some other person or with the right of any person to dispose of his capital or labor.[70]

Section 19 further provides immunity to the agreement between members of the trade union from declaring void[71] or voidable[72] only on the ground of in restraint of trade.[73]

---

[68] Sec.18 of the Trade Union Act, 1926
[69] Both office bearer and members
[70] Sec.18(1) of the Trade Union Act, 1926
[71] Sec.2(g) of the Contract Act, 1872, An agreement not enforceable by law is said to be void
[72] Sec.2(i) of the Contract Act, 1872, An agreement which is enforceable by law at the option of one or more of the parties thereto, but not at the option of the other or others, is a voidable contract.
[73] It provides exception sec.27 of the Contract Act, 1872, Agreement in restraint of trade, void - Every agreement by which anyone is restrained from exercising a lawful profession, trade or business of any kind, is to that extent void.

Right to inspect the account book

The members of the trade union and the office bearer have right to inspect accounts books and the list of the members in the trade union.[74]

Right to minors

Any minor person who has not attained the age of fifteen years can become a member of a registered trade union and shall avail all rights as a member of a trade union.[75]

However, a minor is disqualified to become a member of the executive or an office bearer.[76]

Dissolution

A registered trade union can be dissolved, by giving a notice to the Registrar, signed by any seven members and Secretary of the trade union within fourteen days of the dissolution.

A dissolution shall be registered and shall come to effect from the date of such registration.[77]

---

[74] Sec.20 of the Trade Union Act, 1926
[75] Sec.21 of the Trade Union Act, 1926
[76] Sec. 21A(1)(i) of the Trade Union Act, 1926

If the rules of the trade union do not provide for the distribution of funds on dissolution, the Registrar shall divide the funds, amongst the members in such manner as may be prescribed.[78]

Penalty

A registered trade union if defaults in sending any notice, statement or documents required to sent as per the provisions of the Act, shall be punished with a fine which may extend to five rupees and in the case of a continuing default, with an additional fine which may extend to five rupees for each week.[79]

However, such fine shall not exceed rupees fifty in aggregate. Every office-bearer or other person shall be held responsible and if there is no such office-bearers or person, every member of the executive of the trade union, shall be held responsible for the default.[80]

Any person who provides to any member of a registered trade union or to any person with the intend to deceive, gives any document purporting to be a copy of the rules of the trade union knowing that it is not a correct copy of such rules shall be punished with fine which may extend to two hundred rupees.[81]

---

[77] Sec.27 of the Trade Union Act, 1926
[78] Sec.27(2) of the Trade Union Act, 1926
[79] Sec.31(1) of the Trade Union Act, 1926
[80] Sec.31(2) of the Trade Union Act, 1926
[81] Sec.32 of the Trade Union Act, 1926

Chapter 5

Workman's Compensation

The Workmen's Compensation Act, 1923[82] is one the earliest enactment to provide compensation to workmen in case of death or disability. The Act is applicable to the whole of India and came into effect from July 1924.[83]

In the title of the Act 'Workmen's Compensation Act, 1923 ' the word 'workmen' has been substituted with the word 'Employees' by the Workmen's Compensation (Amendment) Act. 2009.

The Word 'workmen' in the Act, has been substituted with the word 'employees' by the Workmen's Compensation (Amendment) Act. 2009.

Employer's liability for compensation

1) If the personal injury is caused to a workman.

---

[82] http://labour.gov.in/sites/default/files/TheWorkmenAct1923(1).pdf
[83] Sec.1 of the Workmens Compensation Act, 1923

2) The accident must be arising out of and in the course of his employment.

3) If the injury results in the total or partial disablement of the workman.

4) If the injury results in death or permanent total disablement.

Then in such cases, the employer shall be liable to pay compensation in accordance with the provisions of the Act. However, he shall not be liable,

1) If any the injury does not result in disablement[84] for a period exceeding three days.

2) If the injury is caused by an accident which is directly attributable to –

a) That the workman was under the influence of drink or drugs at the time of the accident.

b) Due to willful disobedience of the orders framed for the safety to the workman.

c) Due to willful removal of safety guards or devices.

The term injury includes occupational disease specified in the Part A, Part B and Part C of the Schedule of the Act.[85] An occupational disease are diseases which have contracted as a result of of the exposure to risk factor arising from the work activity.[86]

If a workman contracts an occupational disease, then the employer is liable to pay compensation provided the worker has worked with the employer for a continuous period of six months.[87]

Applicability of the Act

The Act is applicable to workman[88] as given the Act.
Workman means

1) Any person employed other than a person whose employment is of a casual nature and is employed otherwise than for the purposes of the employer's trade or business.

2) Includes a railway servant as defined in Section 3 of the Indian Railways Act 1890.

3) A master seaman and other members of the crew in a ship.

---

[84] In total or partial
[85] Sec.3 of the Workmens Compensation Act, 1923
[86] http://www.who.int/occupational_health/activities/occupational_work_diseases/en/
[87] Sec.3 of the Workmens Compensation Act, 1923
[88] Sec.2n of the Workmens Compensation Act, 1923

4) A captain or other member of the crew in an aircraft.

5) A person recruited as a driver, helper, mechanic, cleaner or in any other capacity in connection with a motor vehicle.

6) A person recruited to work abroad by a company.

7) The employed outside India in any such capacity as is specified in Schedule II.

8) The person employed outside India and the ship, aircraft or motor vehicle or company as the case may be is registered in India.

The concept of workman does not include any member of the Armed Forces of Union. The Schedule II provides a comprehensive list of the nature of employment which is considered as a workman for the purpose of the Act.

Concept of Wages

The concept of wages includes, any benefit which is capable to express in terms of money.

The following is not included in the definition of wages,

1) Travelling allowances

2) Contribution paid by the employer towards any pension.

3) Contribution paid by the employer towards provident fund.

4) Sum paid to a workman for any special expenses necessitate by the nature of his employment.

Chapter 6

Amount of Compensation

Amount of Compensation

The amount of compensation differs from case to case and depends upon the extend of disability suffered by the workman. The compensation claim can be divided into following categories,

1) Death of the workmen

In case of death from the injury an amount equal to fifty percent of the monthly wages of the deceased workman multiplied by the relevant factor or an amount of one lakh and twenty thousand rupees whichever is more.

2) Permanent total disablement

In case of permanent total disablement from the injury an amount equal to sixty percent of the monthly wages of the workman multiplied by the relevant factor or an amount of one lakh and forty thousand rupees whichever is more.

3) Permanent partial disablement

In case of permanent partial disablement of the injury in the case of an injury specified in Part II of Schedule I of the Act, the percentage of the compensation depend on the percentage of the loss of earning capacity caused by the injury.

In the case of an injury specified in Schedule I of the Act, the percentage of the compensation shall be payable in the case of permanent total disablement as is proportionate to the loss of earning capacity as assessed by the qualified medical practitioner.

4) Temporary disablement

In case of temporary disablement whether total or partial, a half monthly payment of the sum equivalent to twenty five percent of the monthly wages of the workman shall paid as compensation to the injured workman.

Contracting

If the work is contracted or the workmen are employed by the contractor then in such case the principal employer shall be responsible to pay compensation as if they were employed by him.[89]

---

[89] Sec.12 of the Workmens Compensation Act, 1923

Notice

A notice shall be served as soon as possible to the employer in case of an accident leading to death or disability and any claim shall be preferred within the period of two years from the date of such occurrence before the Commissioner.

The notice shall be served on the employer or any other responsible to the employer for the management of the business. It shall be sent by a registered post to the employer on the address of the residence, office or place of business.

The Commissioner may allow a claim in case of failure to serve notice or file claim within the prescribed time if satisfied that the failure was due to sufficient cause, thus lack of notice is not a bar to a claim.

The notice shall contain following,

1) Name and address of the injured person.

2) Cause of injury.

3) Date of accident.

Statement on fatal accident

A Commissioner may send notice to the employer on accident resulting in the death of workmen and the required information shall be submitted within 30 days from the service of notice including the opinion of the employer for compensation of the deceased employee. The employer shall deposit compensation within 30 days in case he is of opinion that it is a proper to compensate or else shall submit the cause for refusal of compensation.[90]

Reports of fatal accidents

The employer shall report to the Commissioner any accident causing serious bodily injury[91] or death of workmen within seven days of such incident providing circumstances of such accident.[92]

Reference of Commissioners

The Commissioner shall settle any dispute with regard to the liability of any person to pay compensation, the question whether an injured person is workman or not, extend of disablement.

---

[90] Sec.10A of the Workmens Compensation Act, 1923
[91] "Serious bodily injury" means an injury which involves or in all probability will involve the permanent loss of the use of or permanent injury to any limb or the permanent loss of or injury to the sight or hearing or the fracture of any limb or the enforced absence of the injured person from work for a period exceeding twenty days.
[92] Sec.10B of the Workmens Compensation Act, 1923

There is a bar on jurisdiction of Civil Court to deal with subject matter for which a Commissioner is empowered.[93]

Appointment of Commissioners

The State Government notify in the Official Gazette to appoint any person as the Commissioner for Workmen's Compensation for an area.

Every Commissioner shall be deemed to be a public servant.[94]

Jurisdiction

The matter shall be filled before the Commissioner in an area in which,

a) The place of the accident which resulted in injury.

b) The place of residence of an accident or in case of death of workman the place of residence of the dependant.

c) The place of the registered office of the employer.

Power of Commissioners[95]

---

[93] Sec.19 of the Workmens Compensation Act, 1923
[94] Sec.20 of the Workmens Compensation Act, 1923
[95] Sec.23 of the Workmens Compensation Act, 1923

The Commissioners shall have the power of the Civil Court under the Code of Civil Procedure and shall deemed to be a Civil Court.[96]

---

[96] for all the purposes of section 195 and of Chapter XXVI of the CrPC 1973

Chapter 7

Payment of Wages

The Act, the Payment of Wages Act 1936 is applicable to the whole of India. .It is applicable to the followings,

1) To the persons employed in any factory[97]

2) To the persons employed in any railway by a railway administration.[98]

3) To the persons employed in an industrial establishment.[99]

---

[97] Means a factory as defined in clause (m) of section 2 of the Factories Act 1948 (63 of 1948) and includes any place to which the provisions of that Act have been applied under sub-section (1) of section 85 thereof;

[98] "railway administration" has the meaning assigned to it in clause (6) of section 3 of the Indian Railways Act 1890

4) To other establishment specified in sub-clauses (a) to (g) of clause (ii) of section 2.

The State Government after giving a three months' notice in the Official Gazette, extend the provisions of this Act.

The Act applies to the to an average wage ceiling of INR 18,000 per month.[100]

Responsibility for payment of wages

Section 3 of the Act imposes the responsibility of payment on an employer for the person employed by him. The following have responsibility of payment if they are appointed so,

(a) In factories, the manager of the factory.[101]

---

[99] (a) tramway service or motor transport service engaged in carrying passengers or goods or both by road for hire or reward, (aa) air transport service other than such service belonging to or exclusively employed in the military naval or air forces of the Union or the Civil Aviation Department of the Government of India, (b) dock wharf or jetty, (c) inland vessel mechanically propelled, (d) mine quarry or oil-field, (e) plantation, (f) workshop or other establishment in which articles are produced adapted or manufactured with a view to their use transport or sale, (g) establishment in which any work relating to the construction development or maintenance of buildings roads bridges or canals or relating to operations connected with navigation irrigation or to the supply of water or relating to the generation transmission and distribution of electricity or any other form of power is being carried on, (h) any other establishment or class of establishments which the Central Government or a State Government may having regard to the nature thereof the need for protection of persons employed therein and other relevant circumstances specify by notification in the Official Gazette.

[100] Notification S.O. No.2260(E) Published in the Gazetteof India (extraordinary) part II, Section 3, Sub section (ii), dated 20th September, 2012, Ministry of Labour and Employment, Government of India.

[101] Sec 3(a) of the Payment of Wages Act, 1936

(b) In industrial or other establishments the person responsible to the employer for the supervision and control of the industrial or other establishments.[102]

(c) In railways and if the railway administration has nominated a person for this purpose in a local area concerned.[103]

d) Any other person appointed for this purpose by the employer.

Wage Period

The person responsible for making payment as per section 3 of the Act shall fix a wage period,[104] however such wage periods should not exceed one month.[105]

Time of Payment of wages

In any railway factory or industrial or other establishment upon or were less than a thousand persons are employed, wages shall be paid before the expiry of the seventh day[106] of the wage period and other if more than a thousand persons are employed then it shall be before the expiry of the tenth day[107] of the wage period.

---

[102] Sec 3(b) of the Payment of Wages Act, 1936
[103] Sec 3(c) of the Payment of Wages Act, 1936
[104] Sec 4(1) of the Payment of Wages Act, 1936
[105] Sec 4(2) of the Payment of Wages Act, 1936
[106] Sec 5(1)(a) of the Payment of Wages Act, 1936
[107] Sec 5(1)(b) of the Payment of Wages Act, 1936

In case of termination of employment by the employer, the wages shall be paid before the expiry of the second working day from the day on which his termination of employment.[108]

Payment of wages in current coin or currency notes

All wages shall be paid in current coin or currency notes, including through cheque and payment in the bank account.[109]

---

[108] Sec 5(2) of the Payment of Wages Act, 1936
[109] Sec 6 of the Payment of Wages Act, 1936

Chapter 8

Authorized Deduction from Wages

Authorized deduction from wages

The Act provides that the wages shall be paid without any deduction except of those allowed by the Act. The Act permits following kinds of deduction from the wages,

1) Fines.[110]

2) Deduction for absence from duty.[111]

3) Deduction for damage or loss of goods, however such loss should be as a result of negligence or default on the part of employees.[112]

4) Deduction for housing accommodation when provided by the employer, the Government or any housing board.[113]

---

[110] Sec 7(2)(a) of the Payment of Wages Act, 1936
[111] Sec 7(2)(b) of the Payment of Wages Act, 1936
[112] Sec 7(2)(c) of the Payment of Wages Act, 1936
[113] Sec 7(2)(d) of the Payment of Wages Act, 1936

5) Deduction for amenities, services supplied by the employer as authorized by the Government.[114]

6) Deduction for recovery of advances, interest and for the correction due to over payments of wages.[115]

7) Deduction of recovery of loans provided for the purpose of house building or any other purpose approved by the State Government.[116]

8) Deduction for income tax.[117]

9) Deduction by an order of the Court.[118]

10) Deduction from Provident Funds under the Provident Funds Act 1952 or any provident fund approved by the Government.[119]

11) Deduction for payments to co-operative societies approved by the State Government.[120]

12) Deduction for payment of premium of Insurance policies or securities of the Government of India or of any State Government or for depositing in any Post Office Saving Bank after the prior written authorization of the employed person.[121]

---

[114] Sec 7(2)(e) of the Payment of Wages Act, 1936
[115] Sec 7(2)(f) of the Payment of Wages Act, 1936
[116] Sec 7(2)(fff) of the Payment of Wages Act, 1936

[117] Sec 7(g) of the Payment of Wages Act, 1936
[118] Sec 7(h) of the Payment of Wages Act, 1936
[119] Sec 7(i) of the Payment of Wages Act, 1936
[120] Sec 7(j) of the Payment of Wages Act, 1936
[121] Sec 7(k) of the Payment of Wages Act, 1936

13) Deduction for any fund constituted by the employer or a trade union registered under the Trade Union act 1926.[122]

14) Deduction for payment of fees payable for the membership of any trade union registered under the Trade Union Act 1926.[123]

15) Deductions for payment of insurance premia on Fidelity Guarantee Bonds.[124]

16) Deductions for recovery of losses sustained by a railway administration on acceptance of counterfeit or base coins or mutilated or forged currency notes.[125]

17) Deduction can be made to invoice to bill to collect or to account for the appropriate charges due to the administration in respect of fares freight demurrage wharfage, carnage, sale of food in catering establishments sale of commodities in grain shops or otherwise.[126]

18) Deductions for losses sustained by a railway administration due to any rebates or refunds incorrectly granted by the employed person.[127]

---

[122] Sec 7(kk) of the Payment of Wages Act, 1936

[123] Sec 7(kkk) of the Payment of Wages Act, 1936

[124] Sec 7(l) of the Payment of Wages Act, 1936

[125] Sec 7(m) of the Payment of Wages Act, 1936

[126] Sec 7(n) of the Payment of Wages Act, 1936

[127] Sec 7(o) of the Payment of Wages Act, 1936

19) Deduction for the contribution to the Prime Minister's National Relief Fund or any other as notified by the Central Government in the Official Gazette.[128]

20) Deduction for the contributions to any insurance scheme framed by the Central Government.[129]

Fines

No fine shall be levied on an employee, except for such acts and omission which have been approved by the State Government or by a prescribed authority.[130]

A notice of such acts and omissions shall be exhibited in the prescribed manner on the premises.[131]

No fine shall be imposed without giving an opportunity to show cause against the fine.[132]

The total amount of the fine shall not exceed an amount equal to three percent of the wages in a wage period.[133]

---

[128] Sec 7(p) of the Payment of Wages Act, 1936
[129] Sec 7(q) of the Payment of Wages Act, 1936
[130] Sec 8(1) of the Payment of Wages Act, 1936
[131] Sec 8(2) of the Payment of Wages Act, 1936
[132] Sec 8(3) of the Payment of Wages Act, 1936
[133] Sec 8(4) of the Payment of Wages Act, 1936

No fine shall be imposed on an employee who is below the age of fifteen years.[134]

No fine shall be recovered in instalments and after the expiry of sixty days from the day the fine was imposed.[135]

There shall be a register maintained for record of all fines received and it shall be utilized for the benefit of employed person or as approved by the prescribed authority.[136]

Deductions for absence from duty

A deduction for absence from duty can make when an employee is absent from the place where he is required to work and when such absence is for the whole day or any part of the period during which he is required to work.[137]

If ten or more employees acting in concert absent themselves without giving proper notice and without reasonable cause then in such cases an amount not exceeding their wages for eight days can be deducted in lieu of notice.[138]

---

[134] Sec 8(5) of the Payment of Wages Act, 1936
[135] Sec 8(6) of the Payment of Wages Act, 1936
[136] Sec 8(8) of the Payment of Wages Act, 1936
[137] Sec 9(1) of the Payment of Wages Act, 1936
[138] Sec 9(2) of the Payment of Wages Act, 1936

Deductions for damage or loss

A deduction can be made for the damage or loss caused by an employee by neglect or default on his part, however it shall not exceed the amount of damage.[139] No deduction shall be made without giving a show cause notice against the deduction.[140]

The amount realized through such deduction shall be recorded in a register and shall be kept by the person responsible for the payment of wages.[141]

Deduction for services rendered

A deduction can be made from the wages for the house accommodation amenity or service accepted and such deduction shall not exceed an amount equivalent to the value of the house accommodation amenity or service supplied.[142]

Deduction for recovery of advances

Any recovery of the advance of money which is given before the employment began shall be made from the first payment of wages however no recovery shall be made for travelling expenses.[143]

---

[139] Sec 9(2) of the Payment of Wages Act, 1936
[140] Sec 9(1A) of the Payment of Wages Act, 1936
[141] Sec 10(2) of the Payment of Wages Act, 1936
[142] Sec 11 of the Payment of Wages Act, 1936
[143] Sec 12(a) of the Payment of Wages Act, 1936

The recovery in respect of the amount given after employment began shall be subject to the rules made by the State Government.[144]

Deduction for recovery of loan

Any recovery of loan granted under clause (fff) of the subsection (2) of the section 7 shall be subject to rules made by the State Government.[145]

Registers and Records

The employer shall maintain registers and records providing details of work, wages, deduction made from the wages etc. and such register and record shall be preserved for a period of three years.[146]

---

[144] Sec 12(a) of the Payment of Wages Act, 1936
[145] Sec 12A of the Payment of Wages Act, 1936
[146] Sec 13A of the Payment of Wages Act, 1936

Chapter 9

Inspectors

An Inspector of Factories shall be an Inspector for the purpose of the payment of the Wages Act, 1936 for the local limits assigned to him.[147] Every Inspector shall deemed to be a public servant within the meaning of the Indian Penal Code.[148]

The State Government may appoint an Inspector for railways, factories and industrial or other establishment to which the Act applies.[149] The Inspector may perform the following functions,

1) Examine and make an inquiry to ascertain that the provisions of the Act are being followed.[150]

2) To enter, inspect and search any premises of a railway factory or industrial or other establishment to fulfill the obligation given under the Act.[151]

---

[147] Sec 14(1) of the Payment of Wages Act, 1936
[148] Sec 12(5) of the Payment of Wages Act, 1936
[149] Sec 14(3) of the Payment of Wages Act, 1936
[150] Sec 14(4)(a) of the Payment of Wages Act, 1936
[151] Sec 14(4)(b) of the Payment of Wages Act, 1936

3) To supervise the payments of wages.[152]

4) To order in writing, production of register maintained under the Act and to take statement of persons.[153]

5) To seize or take copies of document, registers or portion of it which he may consider relevant.[154]

6) To exercise other powers which may be prescribed.[155]

The employer shall afford reasonable facilities to Inspectors to enter, inspect, supervise, examine or to make an inquiry under the Act.[156]

---

[152] Sec 14(c) of the Payment of Wages Act, 1936
[153] Sec 14(d) of the Payment of Wages Act, 1936
[154] Sec 14(e) of the Payment of Wages Act, 1936
[155] Sec 14(f) of the Payment of Wages Act, 1936
[156] Sec 14A of the Payment of Wages Act, 1936

¹[***] TRADE UNIONS ACT, 1926

[16 OF 1926]

With State Amendments

An Act to provide for the registration of Trade Unions and in certain respects to define the law relating to registered Trade Unions ²[* *]*

Whereas it is expedient to provide for the registration of Trade Unions and in certain respects to define the law relating to registered Trade Unions; ²[* * *]; it is hereby enacted as follows:—

CHAPTER I

PRELIMINARY

Short title, extent and commencement.

1. (1) This Act may be called ¹[* * *] the Trade Unions Act, 1926.

³[(2) It extends to the whole of India ⁴[* * *],]

(3) It shall come into force on such date as the Central Government may, by notification in the Official Gazette, appoint.

Definitions.

2. In this Act ⁵⁻⁶["the appropriate Government" means, in relation to Trade Unions whose objects are not confined to one State, the Central Government, and in relation to other trade unions, the State Government, and], unless there is anything repugnant in the subject or context,—

(a) "executive" means the body, by whatever name called, to which the management of the affairs of a Trade Union is entrusted;

(b) ⁷[office bearer] in the case of a Trade Union, includes any member of the executive thereof, but does not include an auditor;

(c) "prescribed" means prescribed by regulations made under this Act;

(d) "registered office" means that office of a Trade Union which is registered under this Act as the head office thereof;

(e) "registered Trade Union" means a Trade Union registered under this Act;

[8-9][(*f*) "Registrar" means—

    (*i*) a Registrar of Trade Unions appointed by the appropriate Government under section 3, and includes any Additional or Deputy Registrar of Trade Unions; and

    (*ii*) in relation to any Trade Union, the Registrar appointed for the State in which the head or registered office, as the case may be, of the Trade Union is situated;]

(*g*) "trade dispute" means any dispute between employers and workmen or between workmen and workmen, or between employers and employers which is connected with the employment or non-employment, or the terms of employment or the conditions of labour, of any person, and "workmen" means all persons employed in trade or industry whether or not in the employment of the employer with whom the trade dispute arises; and

(*h*) "Trade Union" means any combination, whether temporary or permanent, formed primarily for the purpose of regulating the relations between workmen and employers or between workmen and workmen, or between employers and employers, or for imposing restrictive conditions on the conduct of any trade or business, and includes any federation of two or more Trade Unions:

Provided that this Act shall not affect—

    (*i*) any agreement between partners as to their own business;

    (*ii*) any agreement between an employer and those employed by him as to such employment; or

    (*iii*) any agreement in considerations of the sale of the goodwill of a business or of instruction in any profession, trade or handicraft.

STATE AMENDMENTS
MADHYA PRADESH

In section 2,

    (*i*) clause (*a*) shall be renumbered as clause (*a-2*) and before clause (*a-2*) as so renumbered the following clauses shall be inserted, namely:—

        "(*a*) 'approved list' means the list of approved unions maintained by the Registrar under section 28A ;

        (a-1) 'approved union' means a registered Trade Union on the approved list;"

    (*ii*) clause (*b*) shall be renumbered as clause (*b-2*) and before clause (*b-2*) as so renumbered, the following clauses shall be inserted, namely:—

"(*b*) 'Industrial Court' shall have the meaning assigned to it in the Madhya Pradesh Industrial Relations Act, 1960 (27 of 1960);"

(*b-1*) [Omitted by MP Act No. 26 of 1981] - *Madhya Pradesh Act No. 28 of 1960.*

CHAPTER II
REGISTRATION OF TRADE UNIONS

Appointment of Registrars

3. [10][(1)] [11][The appropriate Government] shall appoint a person to be the, Registrar of Trade Unions for [12][each State].

[13][(2) The appropriate Government may appoint as many Additional and Deputy Registrars of Trade Unions as it thinks fit for the purpose of exercising and discharging, under the superintendence and direction of the Registrar, such powers and functions of the Registrar under this Act as it may, by order, specify and define the local limits within which any such Additional or Deputy Registrar shall exercise and discharge the powers and functions so specified.

(3) Subject to the provision of any order under sub-section (2), where an Additional or Deputy Registrar exercises and discharges the powers and functions of a Registrar in an area within which the registered office of a Trade Union is situated, the Additional or Deputy Registrar shall be deemed to be the Registrar in relation to the Trade Union for the purposes of this Act.]

Mode of registration.

4. [14][(1) Any seven or more members of a Trade Union may, by subscribing their names to the rules of the Trade Union and by otherwise complying with the provisions of this Act with respect to registration, apply for registration of the Trade Union under this Act:

[14a][**Provided** *that no Trade Union of workmen shall be registered unless at least ten per cent or one hundred of the workmen, whichever is less, engaged or employed in the establishment or industry with which it is connected are the members of such Trade Union on the date of making of application for registration:*

Provided further *that no Trade Union of workmen shall be registered unless it has on the date of making application not less than seven persons as its members, who are workmen engaged or employed in the establishment or industry with which it is connected.*]

[15][(2) Where an application has been made under sub-section (1) for the registration of a Trade Union, such application shall not be deemed to have become invalid merely by reason of the fact that, at any time after the date of the application, but before the registration of the Trade Union, some of the applicants, but not exceeding half of the total number of persons who made the application, have ceased to be members of the Trade Union or have given notice in writing to the Registrar dissociating themselves from the application.]

Application for registration.

5. (1) Every application for registration of a Trade Union shall be made to the Registrar, and shall be accompanied by a copy of the rules of the Trade Union and a statement of the following particulars, namely:—

    (*a*)   the names, occupations and addresses of the members making the application;

[15a][(*aa*) *in the case of a Trade Union of workmen, the names, occupations and addresses of the place of work of the members of the Trade Union making the application;*]

    (*b*)   the name of the Trade Union and the address of its head office; and

    (*c*)   the titles, names, ages, addresses and occupations of the [16][office-bearers] of the Trade Union.

(2) Where a Trade Union has been in existence for more than one year before the making of an application for its registration, there shall be delivered to the Registrar, together with the application, a general statement of the assets and liabilities of the Trade Union prepared in such form and containing such particulars as may be prescribed.

Provisions to be contained in the rules of a Trade Union.

6. A Trade Union shall not be entitled to registration under this Act, unless the executive thereof is constituted in accordance with the provisions of this Act, and the rules thereof provide for the following matters, namely:—

    (*a*)   the name of the Trade Union;

    (*b*)   the whole of the objects for which the Trade Union has been established;

    (*c*)   the whole of the purposes for which the general funds of the Trade Union shall be applicable, all of which purposes shall be purposes to which such funds are lawfully applicable under this Act;

(d) the maintenance of a list of the members of the Trade Union and adequate facilities for the inspection thereof by the [16][office-bearers] and members of the Trade Union;

(e) the admission of ordinary members who shall be persons actually engaged or employed in an industry with which the Trade Union is connected, and also the admission of the number of honorary or temporary members as [16][office-bearers] required under section 22 to form the executive of the Trade Union;

[17][*(ee) the payment of a minimum subscription by members of the Trade Union which shall not be less than—*

    (i) *one rupee per annum for rural workers;*

    (ii) *three rupees per annum for workers in other unorganised sectors; and*

    (iii) *twelve rupees per annum for workers in any other case;*]

(f) the conditions under which any member shall be entitled to any benefit assured by the rules and under which any fine or forfeiture may be imposed on the members;

(g) the manner in which the rules shall be amended, varied or rescinded;

(h) the manner in which the members of the executive and the other [17a][office bearers] of the Trade Union shall be [18][*elected*] and removed;

[18a][*(hh) the duration of period being not more than three years, for which the members of the executive and other office-bearers of the Trade Union shall be elected;*]

(i) the safe custody of the funds of the Trade Union, an annual audit, in such manner as may be prescribed, of the accounts thereof, and adequate facilities for the inspection of the account books by the [17a][office-bearers] and members of the Trade Union; and

(j) the manner in which the Trade Union may be dissolved.

STATE AMENDMENT
MADHYA PRADESH

For clause (*ee*) of section 6, the following clause shall be substituted, namely:—

"(*ee*) the payment of subscription by members of the Trade Union which shall be not less than twenty five paise per month per member:

Provided that the minimum rate of subscription in the case of members of a Trade Union of agricultural workers shall be five paise per month per member" - *Madhya Pradesh Act No. 16 of 1968*

Power to call for further particulars and to require alteration of names.

7. (1) The Registrar may call for further information for the purpose of satisfying himself that any application complies with the provisions of section 5, or that the Trade Union is entitled to registration under section 6, and may refuse to register the Trade Union until such information is supplied.

(2) If the name under which a Trade Union is proposed to be registered is identical with that by which any other existing Trade Union has been registered or, in the opinion of the Registrar, so nearly resembles such name as to be likely to deceive the public or the members of either Trade Union, the Registrar shall require the persons applying for registration to alter the name of the Trade Union stated in the application, and shall refuse to register the Union until such alteration has been made.

Registration.

8. The registrar, on being satisfied that the Trade Union has complied with all the requirements of this Act in regard to registration, shall register the Trade Union by entering in a register, to be maintained in such form as may be prescribed, the particulars relating to the Trade Union contained in the statement accompanying the application for registration.

Certificate of registration.

9. The Registrar, on registering a Trade Union under section 8, shall issue a certificate of registration in the prescribed form which shall be conclusive evidence that the Trade Union has been duly registered under this Act.

[18b][**Minimum requirement about membership of a Trade Union.**

9A. *A registered Trade Union of workmen shall at all times continue to have not less than ten per cent or one hundred of the workmen, whichever is less, subject to a minimum of seven, engaged or employed in an establishment or industry with which it is connected, as its members.*]

Cancellation of registration.

10. A certificate of registration of a Trade Union may be withdrawn or cancelled by the Registrar—

    (*a*)   on the application of the Trade Union to be verified in such manner as may be prescribed, or

(b) if the Registrar is satisfied that the certificate has been obtained by fraud or mistake, or that the Trade Union has ceased to exist or has wilfully and after notice from the Registrar contravened any provisions of this Act or allowed any rule to continue in force which is inconsistent with any such provision, or has rescinded any rule providing for any matter provision for which is required by section 6;

[18b][(c) *if the Registrar is satisfied that a registered Trade Union of workmen ceases to have the requisite number of members:*]

Provided that not less than two months' previous notice in writing specifying the ground on which it is proposed to withdraw or cancel the certificate shall be given by the Registrar to the Trade Union before the certificate is withdrawn or cancelled otherwise than on the application of the Trade Union.

[19][**Appeal.**

11. (1) Any person aggrieved by any refusal of the Registrar to register a Trade Union or by the withdrawal or cancellation of a certificate of registration may, within such period as may be prescribed, appeal—

(a) where the head office of the Trade Union is situated within the limits of a Presidency-town [20][***], to the High Court, or

[20a][(aa) *where the head office is situated in an area, falling within the jurisdiction of a Labour Court or an Industrial Tribunal, to that Court or Tribunal, as the case may be;*]

(b) where the head office is situated in any other area, to such Court, not inferior to the Court of an additional or assistant Judge of a principal Civil Court of original jurisdiction, as the [21][appropriate Government] may appoint in this behalf for that area.

(2) The appellate Court may dismiss the appeal, or pass an order directing the Registrar to register the Union and to issue a certificate of registration under the provisions of section 9 or setting aside the order for withdrawal or cancellation of the certificate, as the case may be, and the Registrar shall comply with such order.

(3) For the purpose of an appeal under sub-section (1) an appellate Court shall, so far as may be, follow the same procedure and have the same powers as it follows and has when trying a suit under the Code of Civil Procedure, 1908 (5 of 1908), and may direct by whom the whole or any part of the costs of the appeal shall be paid, and such costs shall be recovered as if they had been awarded in a suit under the said Code.

(4) In the event of the dismissal of an appeal by any Court appointed under clause (b) of sub-section (1), the person aggrieved shall have a right of appeal to the High Court, and the High Court shall, for the purpose of such appeal, have all the powers of an appellate Court under sub-sections (2) and (3), and the provisions of those sub-sections shall apply accordingly.]

STATE AMENDMENTS
MADHYA PRADESH

For section 11, the following section shall be substituted, namely:—

"11. *Appeal* - (1) Any person aggrieved by an order of the Registrar—

(*a*) refusing to register a trade union; or

(*b*) withdrawing or cancelling a certificate of registration, may within thirty days from the communication of such order to the Trade union concerned, appeal to the Industrial Court whose decision shall be final:

Provided that in computing the period of thirty days, the time required for obtaining a copy of the order shall be excluded.

(2) The Registrar shall comply with any order passed by the industrial Court under sub-section (1)" - *Madhya Pradesh Act No. 28 of 1960*

Registered office.

12. All communications and notices to a registered Trade Union may be addressed to its registered office. Notice of any change in the address of the head office shall be given within fourteen days of such change to the Registrar in writing, and the changed address shall be recorded in the register referred to in section 8.

Incorporation of registered Trade Unions.

13. Every registered Trade Union shall be a body corporate by the name under which it is registered, and shall have perpetual succession and a common seal with power to acquire and hold both movable and immovable property and to contract, and shall by the said name sue and be sued.

Certain Acts not to apply to registered Trade Unions.

14. The following Acts, namely:—

   (*a*) The Societies Registration Act, 1860 (21 of 1860),

   (*b*) The Co-operative Societies Act, 1912 (2 of 1912),

[22][***]

[23][(*c*) The Companies Act, 1956 (1 of 1956),] shall not apply to any registered Trade Union, and the registration of any such Trade Union under any such Act shall be void.

CHAPTER III

RIGHTS AND LIABILITIES OF REGISTERED TRADE UNIONS

Objects on which general funds may be spent.

15. The general funds of a registered Trade Union shall not be spent on any other objects than the following, namely:—

   (*a*) the payment of salaries, allowances and expenses to [24][office-bearers] of the Trade Union;

   (*b*) the payment of expenses for the administration of the Trade Union, including audit of the accounts of the general funds of the Trade Union;

   (*c*) the prosecution or defence of any legal proceeding to which the Trade Union or any member thereof is a party, when such prosecution or defence is undertaken for the purpose of securing or protecting any rights of the Trade Union as such or any rights arising out of the relations of any member with his employer or with a person whom the member employs;

   (*d*) the conduct of trade disputes on behalf of the Trade Union or any member thereof;

   (*e*) the compensation of members for loss arising out of trade disputes;

   (*f*) allowances to members or their dependents on account of death, old age, sickness, accidents or unemployment of such members;

(g) the issue of, of the undertaking of liability under, policies of assurance on the lives of members, or under policies insuring members against sickness, accident or unemployment;

(h) the provisions of educational, social or religious benefits for members (including the payment of the expenses of funeral or religious ceremonies for deceased members) or for the dependents of members;

(i) the upkeep of a periodical published mainly for the purpose of discussing questions affecting employers or workmen as such;

(j) the payment, in furtherance of any of the objects on which the general funds of the Trade Union may be spent, of contributions to any cause intended to benefit workmen in general, provided that the expenditure in respect of such contributions in any financial year shall not at any time during that year be in excess of one-fourth of the combined total of the gross income which has up to that time accrued to the general funds of the Trade Union during that year and of the balance at the credit of those funds at the commencement of that year; and

(k) subject to any conditions contained in the notification, any other object notified by the [25][appropriate Government] in the Official Gazette.

STATE AMENDMENTS
MAHARASHTRA

In Chapter III in the heading, after the words "Trade Unions", the words "and Settlement of Certain Disputes" shall be added—*Maharashtra Act No. 3 of 1968.*

Constitution of a separate fund for political purposes.

16. (1) A registered Trade Union may constitute a separate fund, from contributions separately levied for or made to that fund, from which payments may be made, for the promotion of the civic and political interests of its members, in furtherance of any of the objects specified in sub-section (2).

(2) The objects referred to in sub-section (1) are :—

(a) the payment of any expenses incurred, either directly or indirectly, by a candidate or prospective candidate for election as a member of any legislative body constituted under [26][* * *] [the Constitution] or of any local authority, before, during, or after the election in connection with his candidature or election; or (*b*) the holding of any meeting or the distribution of any literature or documents in support of any such candidate or prospective candidate; or

(*c*) the maintenance of any person who is a member of any legislative body constituted under [26][* * *] [the Constitution] or of any local authority; or

(*d*) the registration of electors or the selection of a candidate for any legislative body constituted under [26][* * *] [the Constitution] or of any local authority; or

(*e*) the holding of political meetings of any kind, or the distribution of political literature or political documents of any kind.

[27][(2A) In its application to the State of Jammu and Kashmir, references in sub-section (2) to any legislative body constituted under the Constitution shall be construed as including references to the Legislature of that State.]

(3) No member shall be compelled to contribute to the fund constituted under sub-section (1); and a member who does not contribute to the said fund shall not be excluded from any benefits of the Trade Union, or placed in any respect either directly or indirectly under any disability or at any disadvantage as compared with other members of the Trade Union (except in relation to the control or management of the said fund) by reason of his not contributing to the said fund; and contribution to the said fund shall not be made a condition for admission to the Trade Union.

Criminal conspiracy in trade disputes.

17. No [28-29][office-bearer] or member of a registered Trade Union shall be liable to punishment under sub-section (2) of section 120B of the Indian Penal Code (45 of 1860), in respect of any agreement made between the members for the purpose of furthering any such object of the Trade Union as is specified in section 15, unless the agreement is an agreement to commit an offence.

Immunity from civil suit in certain cases.

18. (1) No suit or other legal proceeding shall be maintainable in any Civil Court against any registered Trade Union or any [28-29][office-bearer] or member thereof in respect of any act done in contemplation or furtherance of a trade dispute to which a member of the Trade Union is a party on the ground only that such act induces some other person to break a contract of employment, or that it is in interference with the trade, business or employment of some other person or with the right of some other person to dispose of his capital or of his labour as he wills.

(2) A registered Trade Union shall not be liable in any suit or other legal proceeding in any Civil Court in respect of any tortuous act done in contemplation or furtherance of a trade dispute by an agent of the Trade Union if it is proved that such person acted without the knowledge of, or contrary to express instructions given by, the executive of the Trade Union.

Enforceability of agreements.

19. Notwithstanding anything contained in any other law for the time being in force, an agreement between the members of a registered Trade Union shall not be void or voidable merely by reason of the fact that any of the objects of the agreement are in restraint of trade :

Provided that nothing in this section shall enable any Civil Court to entertain any legal proceeding instituted for the express purpose of enforcing or recovering damages for the breach of any agreement concerning the conditions on which any members of a Trade Union shall or shall not sell their goods, transact business, work, employ or be employed.

Right to Inspect books of Trade Union.

20. The account books of a registered Trade Union and the list of members thereof shall be open to inspection by an [28-29][office-bearer] or member of the Trade Union at such times as may be provided for in the rules of the Trade Union.

Rights of minors to membership of Trade Union.

21. Any person who has attained the age of fifteen years may be a member of a registered Trade Union subject to any rules of the Trade Union to the contrary, and may, subject as aforesaid, enjoy all the rights of a member and execute all instruments and give all acquittance necessary to be executed or given under the rules.
[30][* * *]

[31][**Disqualifications of office-bearers of Trade Unions.**

21A. (1) A person shall be disqualified for being chosen as, and for being a member of the executive or any other office-bearer of a registered Trade Union if—

(*i*) he has not attained the age of eighteen years;

(*ii*) he has been convicted by a Court in India of any offence involving moral turpitude and sentenced to imprisonment, unless a period of five years has elapsed since his release.

(2) Any member of the executive or other office-bearer of a registered Trade Union who, before the commencement of the Indian Trade Unions (Amendment) Act, 1964, has been convicted of any offence involving moral turpitude and sentenced to imprisonment, shall on the date of such commencement cease to be such member or office-bearer unless a period of five years has elapsed since his release before that date.]

[32][(3) In its application to the State of Jammu and Kashmir, reference in sub-section (2) to the commencement of the Indian Trade Unions (Amendment) Act, 1964 (38 of 1964), shall be construed as reference to the commencement of this Act in the said State.]

[33-34][**Proportion of office-bearers to be connected with the industry.**

22. *(1) Not less than one-half of the total number of the office-bearers of every registered Trade Union in an unorganised sector shall be persons actually engaged or employed in an industry with which the Trade Union is connected:*

Provided *that the appropriate Government may, by special or general order, declare that the provisions of this section shall not apply to any Trade Union or class of Trade Unions specified in the order.*

Explanation. —For the purposes of this section, "unorganised sector" means any sector which the appropriate Government may, by notification in the Official Gazette, specify.

(2) Save as otherwise provided in sub-section (1), all office-bearers of a registered Trade Union, except not more than one-third of the total number of the office-bearers or five, whichever is less, shall be persons actually engaged or employed in the establishment or industry with which the Trade Union is connected.

Explanation.—For the purposes of this sub-section, an employee who has retired or has been retrenched shall not be construed as outsider for the purpose of holding an office in a Trade Union.

(3) No member of the Council of Ministers or a person holding an office of profit (not being an engagement or employment in an establishment or industry with which the Trade Union is connected), in the Union or a State, shall be a member of the executive or other office-bearer of a registered Trade Union.]

Change of name.

23. Any registered Trade Union may, with the consent of not less than two-thirds of the total number of its members and subject to the provisions of section 25, change its name.

Amalgamation of Trade Unions.

24. Any two or more registered Trade Unions may become amalgamated together as one Trade Union with or without dissolution or division of the funds of such Trade Union or either or any of them, provided that the votes of at least one-half of the members of each or every such Trade Union entitled to vote are recorded, and that at least sixty per cent of the votes recorded are in favour of the proposal.

Notice of change of name or amalgamation.

25. (1) Notice in writing of every change of name and of every amalgamation, signed, in the case of a change of name, by the Secretary and by seven members of the Trade Union changing its name, and, in the case of an amalgamation, by the Secretary and by seven members of each and every Trade Union which is a party thereto, shall be sent to the Registrar, and where the head office of the amalgamated Trade Union is situated in a different State, to the Registrar of such State.

(2) If the proposed name is identical with that by which any other existing Trade Union has been registered or, in the opinion of the Registrar, so nearly resembles such name as to be likely to deceive the public or the members of either Trade Union, the Registrar shall refuse to register the change of name.

(3) Save as provided in sub-section (2), the Registrar shall, if he is satisfied that the provisions of this Act in respect of change of name have been complied with, register the change of name in the register referred to in section 8, and the change of name shall have effect from the date of such registration.

(4) The Registrar of the State in which the head office of the amalgamated Trade Union is situated shall, if he is satisfied that the provisions of this Act in respect of amalgamation have been complied with and that the Trade Union formed thereby is entitled to registration under section 6, register the Trade Union in the manner provided in section 8, and the amalgamation shall have effect from the date of such registration.

Effects of change of name and of amalgamation.

26. (1) The change in the name of a registered Trade Union shall not affect any rights or obligations of the Trade Union or render defective any legal proceeding by or against the Trade Union, and any legal proceeding which might have been continued or commenced by or against it by its former name may be continued or commenced by or against it by its new name.

(2) An amalgamation of two or more registered Trade Unions shall not prejudice any right of any of such Trade Unions or any right of a creditor of any of them.

Dissolution.

27. (1) When a registered Trade Union is dissolved, notice of the dissolution signed by seven members and by the Secretary of the Trade Union shall, within fourteen days of the dissolution, be sent to the Registrar, and shall be registered by him if he is satisfied that the dissolution has been effected in accordance with the rules of the Trade Union, and the dissolution shall have effect from the date of such registration.

(2) Where the dissolution of a registered Trade Union has been registered and the rules of the Trade Union do not provide of the distribution of funds of the Trade Union on dissolution, the Registrar shall divide the funds amongst the members in such manner as may be prescribed.

Returns.

28. (1) There shall be sent annually to the Registrar, on or before such date as may be prescribed, a general statement, audited in the prescribed manner, of all receipts and expenditure of every registered Trade Union during the year ending on the 31st day of [35][December] next preceding such prescribed date, and of the assets and liabilities of the Trade Union existing on such 31st day of [35][December]. The statement shall be prepared in such form and shall comprise such particulars as may be prescribed.

(2) Together with the general statement there shall be sent to the Registrar a statement showing all changes of [36][office-bearers] made by the Trade Union during the year to which the general statement refers, together also with a copy of the rules of the Trade Union corrected up to the date of the despatch thereof to the Registrar.

(3) A copy of every alteration made in the rules of a registered Trade Union shall be sent to the Registrar within fifteen days of the making of the alteration.

[37][(4) For the purpose of examining the documents referred to in sub-sections (1), (2) and (3), the Registrar, or any officer authorised by him, by general or special order, may at all reasonable times inspect the certificate of registration, account books, registers, and other documents, relating to a Trade Union, at its registered office or may require their production at such place as he may specify, in this behalf, but no such place shall be at a distance of more than ten miles from the registered office of a Trade Union.]

STATE AMENDMENTS

MAHARASHTRA

In Chapter III, after section 28, the following new section shall be inserted, namely :—

"**28A.** *Power of Industrial Court to decide certain disputes.*—(1) When there is a dispute as respects whether or not any person is an office-bearer or member of a registered Trade Union (including any dispute relating to a wrongful expulsion of any such office-bearer or member), or where there is any dispute relating to the property (including the account books) of any registered Trade Union, any member of such registered Trade Union for a period of not less than six months may, with the consent of the Registrar, and in such manner as may be prescribed, refer the dispute to the Industrial Court constituted under the Bombay Industrial Relations Act, 1946, for decision.

(2) The Industrial Court shall, after hearing the parties to the dispute decide the dispute; and may require an office-bearer or member of the registered Trade Union, to be appointed whether by election or otherwise under the supervision of such person as the Industrial Court may appoint in this behalf or removed, in accordance with the rules of the Trade Union :

Provided that, the Industrial Court may, pending the decision of the dispute, make an interim order specifying or appointing any person or appointing a committee of Administration for any purpose under the Act including the purpose of taking possession or control of the property in dispute and managing it for the purposes of the Union pending the decision.

(3) The decision of the Industrial Court shall be final and binding on the parties, and shall not be called in question in any civil court.

(4) No civil court shall entertain any suit or other proceedings in relation to the dispute referred to the Industrial Court as aforesaid, and if any suit or proceeding is pending in any such court, the civil court shall, on receipt of an intimation from the Industrial Court that it is seized of the question, cease exercise jurisdiction in respect thereof.

(5) Save as aforesaid, the Industrial Tribunal may, in deciding dispute under this section, exercise the same powers and follow the same procedure as it exercises or follows for the purpose of deciding industrial disputes under the Bombay Industrial Relations Act, 1946."—*vide Maharashtra Act No. 3 of 1968.*

MADHYA PRADESH

After Chapter III of the Principal Act, the following Chapter shall be inserted namely :—

'CHAPTER III-A
APPROVED UNIONS

28A. *Maintenance of list of Approved Unions.*—It shall be the duty of the Registrar to maintain in such form as may be prescribed a list of approved unions.

28B. *Certain unions deemed to be approved unions.*—A union entered on the approved list maintained under the Bombay Industrial Relations Act, 1947, as adapted in Madhya Bharat by the Madhya Bharat Industrial Relations (Adaptation) Act [Samvat 2006 (31 of 1949)], before the commencement of the Indian Trade Unions (Madhya Pradesh Amendment) Act, 1960 (28 of 1960), shall be deemed to be an approved union under this Act.

28C. *Application for and entry in the approved list.*—(1) Any representative Union or where there is no representative Union any registered Trade Union in any industry other than an industry for which the Central Government is the appropriate Government within the meaning of sub-clause (i) of clause *(a) of* section 2 of the Industrial Disputes Act, 1947 (14 of 1947), may apply in the prescribed form for being entered in the approved list.

(2) On receipt of such application the Registrar shall hold such enquiry as is prescribed and if he is satisfied that such union fulfils the conditions necessary for its being entered in the approved list, he shall enter the name of such union in the approved list and shall issue a certificate of its entry in such form as may be prescribed :

Provided that—

(*i*) where two or more unions fulfilling the conditions necessary for registration specified in section 28D apply for their entry in the approved list, the Union which has the largest membership of the employees employed in the industry, shall alone be entered in the approved list;

(*ii*) the Registrar shall not enter any union in the approved list, if he is satisfied for reasons to be recorded in writing that the application for entry is not made *bona fide* in the interests of employees but is made in the interests of the employer.

Explanation: For the purposes of this section, the expression "Representative Union" shall have the meaning assigned to it in the Madhya Pradesh Industrial Relations Act, 1960 (27 of 1960).

28D. *Conditions of entry in the approved list.*—(1) No union shall be entered in the approved list under this Act, unless—

(*i*) the union has for the whole of the period of three months next preceding the date of application under section 28C a membership of not less than fifteen per cent of the employees employed in the industry in that local area;

(*ii*) the constitution of the union shall be such as may be provided by or under this Act, and in particular, shall require that—

(*a*) the subscription payable for membership shall be not less than four annas a month or such other sum as may be fixed by the State Government under sub-section (2) and that the accounts of the union shall be audited at least once in each financial year by an auditor appointed or approved by the State Government;

(*b*) the executive of the union shall meet at least once in three months and that all resolutions passed by the executive or general body shall be recorded in a minute book; and

(*c*) the union shall not sanction a strike as long as conciliation and arbitration are available and shall not declare a strike until a ballot is taken and the majority of the members of the union vote in favour of the strikes.

(2) The State Government may, by notification, direct that in the case of any registered trade union or workmen or employees engaged in employment specified in the schedule to the Minimum Wages Act, 1948 (XI of 1948), the membership subscription may be less than four annas for such period as may be specified therein.

(3) Any registered Trade Union complying with the conditions specified in sub-section (1) and having a larger membership in an industry in a local area than an approved union for such industry shall on an application in that behalf be entered in the approved list in place of such approved union by the Registrar after holding such enquiry as he deems fit.

28E. *Approved union to continue to be so for altered local area for sometime.*—Notwithstanding anything contained in section 28D, if there is any alteration in the local area or areas—

(*a*)   an approved union in an industry in the altered local area or areas; or

(*b*)   where two or more approved unions exist in an industry in the altered local area or areas, the union having the largest membership, whether by agreement of the other approved unions or as determined by the registrar after such inquiry as he deems fit;

shall be deemed to be the approved union for the altered local area or areas, as the case may be, for a period of six months from the date on which such alteration is effected or where such approved union or any other union in the altered local area or areas makes an application under section 28C within such period until the disposal of such application by the Registrar.

28F. *Removal from approved list.*—The Registrar shall remove a union from the approved list if its certificate of registration is cancelled under section 10, and may also so remove a union if after holding such enquiry, as he deems fit, he is satisfied that it—

(*i*)   was entered in the list under mistake, misrepresentation or fraud; or

(*ii*)   has, since being included in the approved list, ceased to fulfil the conditions specified in section 28D.

28G. *Appeal.*—(1) Any person aggrieved by the order of the Registrar—

(*a*)   refusing to enter any registered trade union in the approved list; or

(*b*)   removing a registered trade union from the approved list;

may, within thirty days from the communication of such order to the trade union concerned, appeal to the Industrial Court whose decision shall be final:

Provided that in computing the period of thirty days the period requisite for obtaining a copy of the order shall be excluded.

(2) The Registrar shall comply with any order passed by the industrial Court under sub-section (1).

28H. *Rights of officer of approved unions.*—Such officers and members of an approved union as may be authorised by or under rules made in this behalf by the State Government, shall, in such manner and subject to such conditions as may be prescribed, have a right—

(a) to collect sums payable by members to the union on the premises where wages are paid to them;

(b) to put up or cause to be put up a notice board in the premises of the undertaking in which its members are employed and affix or cause to be affixed notices thereon;

(c) for the purpose of the prevention or settlement of a trade dispute—

   (i) to hold discussions on the premises of the undertaking with the employees concerned who are the members of the union;

   (ii) to meet and discuss with an employer or any person appointed by him for the purpose of removing the grievances of its members employed in his undertaking;

   (iii) to inspect, if necessary, in any undertaking; any place where any member of the union is employed.

28HH. *Definitions.*—In this Chapter,—

(a) "Industry" shall have the meaning assigned to that expression in the Madhya Pradesh Industries Relations Act, 1960 (27 of 1960).

(b) 'local area' means any area, notified by the Registrar as a local area for any or all industries for the purposes of this Chapter.

28-I. *Other powers of Registrar.*—(1) For the purposes of discharging his duties generally under the Act and verifying the correctness of the annual returns submitted under section 28, the Registrar shall have power to inspect the account books, the list of members and the minute book of a registered Trade Union :

Provided that an inspection made under this sub-section shall, as far as practicable, be done at the office of the registered Trade Union or at a place within a reasonable distance therefrom and after giving reasonable notice.

(2) For the purposes of discharging his duties under Chapter III-A, the Registrar shall, in addition to the powers mentioned in sub-section (1), have—

(a) the following powers of a court of civil jurisdiction under the Code of Civil Procedure, 1908 (5 of 1908), namely—

   (i) power to require or accept the proof of facts by affidavits;

   (ii) power to summon and enforce the attendance of any person and to examine him on oath;

   (iii) power to compel the production of documents; and

   (iv) power to issue commission for the examination of witnesses;

(*b*) power to enter and inspect any place used by a registered Trade Union as office after giving reasonable notice; and

(*c*) such other powers as may be prescribed.

28J. *Dispute as to officer of registered Trade Union.*—(1) If there is any dispute as to who is the lawful officer of a registered Trade Union, any person claiming to be such an officer or the Registrar may refer the dispute to the Industrial Court in such manner and on payment of such fee not exceeding ten rupees as may be prescribed :

Provided that no fees shall be payable by Registrar.

(2) On a reference being made under sub-section (1), the Industrial Court shall, after hearing the parties to such dispute and recording such evidence as it may consider necessary, decide the dispute and declare who is the lawful officer. The decision of the Industrial Court shall be final and shall not be called in question in any court of law.

(2A) The costs of and incidental to the proceedings under this section shall be in the discretion of the Industrial Court and the Industrial Court shall have full power to determine by whom the whole or any part of such costs shall be paid.

(2B) If in any proceeding under this section, the Industrial Court is, after hearing the person making the reference, satisfied that the ground on which the claim has been preferred is false or vexatious, the Court may after recording its reasons for holding such claim to be false or vexatious, make an order for the payment of costs by way of compensation which shall not be less than fifty rupees and not exceeding two hundred rupees to such person or persons, as it may specify in the order.

(3) No civil court shall entertain any suit or other proceedings in respect of any dispute which has been referred to the Industrial Court under sub-section (1) and is pending before such Court and if any such suit or proceeding is pending in a civil court on the date of the reference, the civil court shall, on receipt of a notice from the Industrial Court, cease to exercise jurisdiction in respect thereof and shall forthwith transfer the record such suit or proceeding to the Industrial Court.

28K. *Certain officers to be public servants.*—The Registrar, Additional Registrar and Deputy Registrar of Trade Unions appointed under section 3 and members of the staff of the offices of the aforesaid officers shall be deemed to be public servants within the meaning of section 21 of the Indian Penal Code, 1860 (45 of 1860).

28L. *Protection of action under the Act.*—No suit, prosecution or legal proceeding shall lie against any person for anything which is in good faith done or purported to be done under this Act.' - *Madhya Pradesh Act No. 28 of 1960, 16 of 1968, 11 of 1963 and 26 of 1981.*

CHAPTER IV
REGULATIONS

Power to make regulations.

29. (1) [38][***] The [39][appropriate Government] may make regulations for the purpose of carrying into effect the provisions of this Act.

(2) In particular and without prejudice to the generality of the forgoing power, such regulations may provide for all or any of the following matters, namely:—

(*a*) the manner in which Trade Unions and the rules of Trade Unions shall be registered and the fees payable on registration;

(*b*) the transfer of registration in the case of any registered Trade Union which has changed its head office from one State to another;

(*c*) the manner in which, and the qualifications of persons by whom, the accounts of registered Trade Unions or of any class of such Unions shall be audited;

(*d*) the conditions subject to which inspection of documents kept by Registrars shall be allowed and the fees which shall be chargeable in respect of such inspections; and

(*e*) any matter which is to be or may be prescribed.

[39a][*(3) Every notification made by the Central Government under sub-section (1) of section 22, and every regulation made by it under sub-section (1), shall be laid, as soon as may be after it is made, before each House of Parliament, while it is in session, for a total period of thirty days which may be comprised in one session or in two or more successive sessions, and if, before the expiry of the session immediately following the session or the successive sessions aforesaid, both Houses agree in making any modification in the notification or regulation, or both Houses agree that the notification or regulation should not be made, the notification or regulation shall thereafter have effect only in such modified form or be of no effect, as the case may be; so, however, that any such modification or annulment shall be without prejudice to the validity of anything previously done under that notification or regulation.*

(4) Every notification made by the State Government under sub-section (1) of section 22 and every regulation made by it under sub-section (1) shall be laid, as soon as may be after it is made, before the State Legislature.]

STATE AMENDMENTS
MAHARASHTRA

In sub-section (2), in clause *(d)*, the word "and" shall be deleted, and after clause (d), the following new clause shall be inserted, namely:—

"*(dd)*   the manner in which the dispute may be referred to the Industrial Court under section *28-IA;"—Maharashtra Act No. 3 of 1968.*

MADHYA PRADESH

In section 29 for the heading of Chapter IV the word "Miscellaneous" shall be substituted for "Regulations".

After clause *(d)* the following clauses shall be inserted, namely:—

"*(d-1)*   the form in which the approved list shall be maintained under section 28A;

(d-2)   the form of application under section 28C;

(d-3)   the officers and members of approved unions to be authorised under section 28H and the manner in which and the conditions subject to which the rights of such officers under that section shall be exercised;

(d-4)   the manner of enquiry required to be undertaken by the Registrar under this Act;

(*d-5*) the manner in which the dispute shall be referred to Industrial Court and the fee payable therefor under section 28J" - *Madhya Pradesh Act Nos. 28 of 1960 and 11 of 1963*.

Publication of regulations.

30. (1) The power to make regulations conferred by section 29 is subject to the condition of the regulations being made after previous publication.

(2) The date to be specified in accordance with clause (3) of section 23 of the General Clauses Act, 1897 (10 of 1897), as that after which a draft of regulations proposed to be made will be taken into consideration shall not be less than three months from the date on which the draft of the proposed regulations was published for general information.

(3) Regulations so made shall be published in the Official Gazette, and on such publication shall have effect as if enacted in this Act.

CHAPTER V
PENALTIES AND PROCEDURE

Failure to submit returns.

31. (1) If default is made on the part of any registered Trade Union in giving any notice or sending any statement or other document as required by or under any provision of this Act, every [40][office-bearer] or other person bound by the rules of the Trade Union to give or send the same, or, if there is no such [40][office-bearer] or person, every member of the executive of the Trade Union, shall be punishable with fine which may extend to five rupees and, in the case of a continuing default, with an additional fine which may extend to five rupees for each week after the first during which the default continues :

Provided that the aggregate fine shall not exceed fifty rupees.

(2) Any person who wilfully makes, or causes to be made, any false entry in, or any omission from, the general statement required by section 28, or in or from any copy of rules or of alterations of rules sent to the Registrar under that section, shall be punishable with fine which may extend to five hundred rupees.

Supplying false information regarding Trade Unions.

32. Any person who, with intent to deceive, gives to any member of a registered Trade Union or to any person intending or applying to become a member of such Trade Union any document purporting to be a copy of the rules of the Trade Union or of any alterations to the same which he knows, or has reason to believe, is not a correct copy of such rules or alteration as are for the time being in force, or any person who, with the like intent, gives a copy of any rules of an unregistered Trade Union to any person on the pretence that such rules are the rules of a registered Trade Union, shall be punishable with fine which may extend to two hundred rupees.

STATE AMENDMENTS
MADHYA PRADESH

After section 32 the following section shall be inserted namely:—

"32A. *Penalty for contravention of section 28H.*—Any employer who contravenes the provisions of section 28H shall be punishable with fine which may extend to five hundred rupees". - *Madhya Pradesh Act No. 28 of 1960.*

Cognizance of offences.

33. (1) No Court inferior to that of a Presidency Magistrate or a Magistrate of the first class shall try any offence under this Act.

(2) No Court shall take cognizance of any offence under this Act, unless complaint thereof has been made by, or with the previous sanction of, the Registrar or, in the case of an offence under section 32, by the person to whom the copy was given, within six months of the date on which the offence is alleged to have been committed.

STATE AMENDMENTS
MAHARASHTRA

In section 33 of the Indian Trade Unions Act, 1926, to sub-section (2) the following shall be added, namely:—

"and in the case of an offence under sub-section (2) of section 31 within six months next after the alleged offence came to the knowledge of the Registrar" - *Maharashtra Act No. XXXII of 1956.*

s

***

EMPLOYEES' COMPENSATION ACT, 1923

[8 OF 1923]

An Act to provide for the payment by certain classes of employers to their employees of compensation for injury by accident.

WHEREAS it is expedient to provide for the payment by certain classes of employers to their employees of compensation for injury by accident; it is hereby enacted as follows:—

CHAPTER I
PRELIMINARY

Short title, extent and commencement.

1. (1) This Act may be called the *Employee's* Compensation Act, 1923.

(2) It extends to the whole of India.

(3) It shall come into force on the first day of July, 1924.

Definitions.

2. (1) In this Act, unless there is anything repugnant in the subject or context,—

(*a*) [* * *]

(*b*) "Commissioner" means a Commissioner for *employees'* Compensation appointed under section 20;

(*c*) "compensation" means compensation as provided for by this Act;

(*d*) "dependant" means any of the following relatives of a deceased *employee*, namely:—

    (*i*) a widow, a minor legitimate or adopted son, and unmarried legitimate or adopted] daughter, or a widowed mother; and

    (*ii*) if wholly dependent on the earnings of the *employee* at the time of his death, a son or a daughter who has attained the age of 18 years and who is infirm;

    (*iii*) if wholly or in part dependent on the earnings of the *employee* at the time of his death,

        (*a*) a widower,

        (*b*) a parent other than a widowed mother,

(c) a minor illegitimate son, an unmarried illegitimate daughter or a daughter legitimate or illegitimate or adopted if married and a minor or if widowed and a minor,

(d) a minor brother or an unmarried sister or a widowed sister if a minor,

(e) a widowed daughter-in-law,

(f) a minor child of a pre-deceased son,

(g) a minor child of a pre-deceased daughter where no parent of the child is alive, or

(h) a paternal grandparent if no parent of the *employee* is alive.

Explanation.—For the purposes of sub-clause (*ii*) and items (*f*) and (*g*) of sub-clause (*iii*), references to a son, daughter or child include an adopted son, daughter or child respectively;

(dd) *"employee"* means a person, who is—

(i) a railway servant as defined in clause (34) of section 2 of the Railways Act, 1989 (24 of 1989), not permanently employed in any administrative district or sub-divisional office of a railway and not employed in any such capacity as is specified in Schedule II; or

(ii) (a) *a master, seaman or other members of the crew of a ship,*

(b) *a captain or other member of the crew of an aircraft,*

(c) *a person recruited as driver, helper, mechanic, cleaner or in any other capacity in connection with a motor vehicle,*

(d) *a person recruited for work abroad by a company,*

and who is employed outside India in any such capacity as is specified in Schedule II and the ship, aircraft or motor vehicle, or company, as the case may be, is registered in India; or

(iii) *employed in any such capacity as is specified in Schedule II, whether the contract of employment was made before or after the passing of this Act and whether such contract is expressed or implied, oral or in writing; but does not include any person working in the capacity of a member of the Armed Forces of the Union; and any reference to any employee who has been injured shall, where the employee is dead, include a reference to his dependants or any of them;*

(*e*) "employer" includes any body of persons whether incorporated or not and any managing agent of an employer and the legal representative of a deceased employer, and, when the services of an *employee* are temporarily lent or let on hire to another person by the person with whom the *employee* has entered into a contract of service or apprenticeship, means such other person while the *employee* is working for him;

(*f*) "managing agent" means any person appointed or acting as the representative of another person for the purpose of carrying on such other person's trade or business, but does not include an individual manager subordinate to an employer;

(*ff*) "minor" means a person who has not attained the age of 18 years;

(*g*) "partial disablement" means, where the disablement is of a temporary nature, such disablement as reduces the earning capacity of a workman in any employment in which he was engaged at the time of the accident resulting in the disablement, and, where the disablement is of a permanent nature, such disablement as reduces his earning capacity in every employment which he was capable of undertaking at that time:

Provided that every injury specified in Part II of Schedule I shall be deemed to result in permanent partial disablement;

(*h*) "prescribed" means prescribed by rules made under this Act;

(*i*) "qualified medical practitioner" means any person registered under any Central Act, Provincial Act, or an Act of the Legislature of a State providing for the maintenance of a register of medical practitioners, or, in any area where no such last-mentioned Act is in force, any person declared by the State Government, by notification in the Official Gazette, to be a qualified medical practitioner for the purposes of this Act;

[* * *]

(k) "seaman" means any person forming part of the crew of any ship, but does not include the master of the ship;

(l) "total disablement" means such disablement, whether of a temporary or permanent nature, as incapacitates an *employee* for all work which he was capable of performing at the time of the accident resulting in such disablement :

Provided that permanent total disablement shall be deemed to result from every injury specified in Part I of Schedule I or from any combination of injuries specified in Part II thereof where the aggregate percentage of the loss of earning capacity, as specified in the said Part II against those injuries, amounts to one hundred per cent or more;

(m) "wages' includes any privilege or benefit which is capable of being estimated in money, other than a travelling allowance or the value of any travelling concession or a contribution paid by the employer an *employee* towards any pension or provident fund or a sum paid to an *employee* to cover any special expenses entailed on him by the nature of his employment;

(n) [***]

(2) The exercise and performance of the powers and duties of a local authority or of any department acting on behalf of the Government shall, for the purposes of this Act, unless a contrary intention appears, be deemed to be the trade or business of such authority or department.

(3) The Central Government or the State Government, by notification in the Official Gazette, after giving not less than three months' notice of its intention so to do, may, by a like notification, add to Schedule II any class of persons employed in any occupation which it is satisfied is a hazardous occupation, and the provisions of this Act shall thereupon apply, in case of a notification by the Central Government, within the territories to which the Act extends, or, in the case of a notification by the State Government, within the State, to such classes of persons :

Provided that in making addition, the Central Government or the State Government, as the case may be, may direct that the provisions of this Act shall apply to such classes of persons in respect of specified injuries only.

CHAPTER II
EMPLOYEES' COMPENSATION

Employer's liability for compensation.

3. (1) If personal injury is caused to an *employee* by accident arising out of and in the course of his employment, his employer shall be liable to pay compensation in accordance with the provisions of this Chapter:

Provided that the employer shall not be so liable—

(*a*) in respect of any injury which does not result in the total or partial disablement of the *employee* for a period exceeding three days;

(*b*) in respect of any [injury, not resulting in death or permanent total disablement, caused by an accident which is directly attributable to—

(*i*) the *employee* having been at the time thereof under the influence of drink or drugs, or

(*ii*) the wilful disobedience of the *employee* to an order expressly given, or to a rule expressly framed, for the purpose of securing the safety of *employees*, or

(*iii*) the wilful removal or disregard by the *employee* of any safety guard or other device which he knew to have been provided for the purpose of securing the safety of *employees*,

(2) If an *employee* employed in any employment specified in Part A of Schedule III contracts any disease specified therein as an occupational disease peculiar to that employment, or if an *employee*, whilst in the service of an employer in whose service he has been employed for a continuous period of not less than six months (which period shall not include a period of service under any other employer in the same kind of employment) in any employment specified in Part B of Schedule III, contracts any disease specified therein as an occupational disease peculiar to that employment, or if an *employee* whilst in the service of one or more employers in any employment specified in Part C of Schedule III, for such continuous period as the Central Government may specify in respect of each such employment, contracts any disease specified therein as an occupational disease peculiar to that employment, the contracting of the disease shall be deemed to be an injury by accident within the meaning of this section and, unless the contrary is proved, the accident shall be deemed to have arisen out of, and in the course of, the employment:

Provided that if it is proved,—

 (*a*) that an *employee* whilst in the service of one or more employers in any employment specified in Part C of Schedule III has contracted a disease specified therein as an occupational disease peculiar to that employment during a continuous period which is less than the period specified under this sub-section for that employment, and

 (*b*) that the disease has arisen out of and in the course of the employment;

the contracting of such disease shall be deemed to be an injury by accident within the meaning of this section :

Provided further that if it is proved that an *employee* who having served under any employer in any employment specified in Part B of Schedule III or who having served under one or more employers in any employment specified in Part C of that Schedule, for a continuous period specified under this sub-section for that employment and he has after the cessation of such service contracted any disease specified in the said Part B or the said Part C, as the case may be, as an occupational disease peculiar to the employment and that such disease arose out of the employment, the contracting of the disease shall be deemed to be an injury by accident within the meaning of this section.

(2A) If an *employee* employed in any employment specified in Part C of Schedule III contracts any occupational disease peculiar to that employment, the contracting whereof is deemed to be an injury by accident within the meaning of this section, and such employment was under more than one employer, all such employers shall be liable for the payment of the compensation in such proportion as the Commissioner may, in the circumstances, deem just.

(3) The Central Government or the State Government], after giving, by notification in the Official Gazette, not less than three months' notice of its intention so to do, may, by a like notification, add any description of employment to the employments specified in Schedule III, and shall specify in the case of employments so added the diseases which shall be deemed for the purposes of this section to be occupational diseases peculiar to those employments respectively, and thereupon the provisions of sub-section (2) shall apply, in the case of a notification by the Central Government, within the territories to which this Act extends or, in case of a notification by the State Government, within the State as if such diseases had been declared by this Act to be occupational diseases peculiar to those employments.

(4) Save as provided by sub-sections (2), (2A) and (3), no compensation shall be payable to an *employee* in respect of any disease unless the disease is directly attributable to a specific injury by accident arising out of and in the course of his employment.

(5) Nothing herein contained shall be deemed to confer any right to compensation on an *employee* in respect of any injury if he has instituted in a Civil Court a suit for damages in respect of the injury against the employer or any other person; and no suit for damages shall be maintainable by an *employee* in any Court of law in respect of any injury—

 (*a*) if he has instituted a claim to compensation in respect of the injury before a Commissioner; or

 (*b*) if an agreement has been come to between the *employee* and his employer providing for the payment of compensation in respect of the injury in accordance with the provisions of this Act.

Amount of compensation.

4. (1) Subject to the provisions of this Act, the amount of compensation shall be as follows, namely :—

(*a*)	where death results from the injury	an amount equal to fifty per cent of the monthly wages of the deceased *employee* multiplied by the relevant factor;
		or
		an amount of *one lakh and twenty thousand rupees*,
		whichever is more;
(*b*)	where permanent total disablement results from the injury	an amount equal to sixty per cent of the monthly wages of the injured *employee* multiplied by the relevant factor;
		or
		an amount of *one lakh and forty thousand rupees*,
		whichever is more.

Explanation I: For the purposes of clause (*a*) and clause (*b*), "relevant factor", in relation to an *employee* means the factor specified in the second column of Schedule IV against the entry in the first column of that Schedule specifying the number of years which are the same as the completed years of the age of the *employee* on his last birthday immediately preceding the date on which the compensation fell due.

Explanation II: [***];

Provided *that the Central Government may, by notification in the Official Gazette, from time to time, enhance the amount of compensation mentioned in clauses (*a*) and (*b*);*

(*c*)	where permanent partial disablement results from the injury	(*i*)	in the case of an injury specified in Part II of Schedule I, such percentage of the compensation which would have been payable in the case of permanent total

disablement as is specified therein as being the percentage of the loss of earning capacity caused by that injury, and

(*ii*) in the case of an injury not specified in Schedule I, such percentage of the compensation payable in the case of permanent total disablement as is proportionate to the loss of earning capacity (as assessed by the qualified medical practitioner) permanently caused by the injury.

Explanation I: Where more injuries than one are caused by the same accident, the amount of compensation payable under this head shall be aggregated but not so in any case as to exceed the amount which would have been payable if permanent total disablement had resulted from the injuries.

Explanation II: In assessing the loss of earning capacity for the purposes of sub-clause (ii) the qualified medical practitioner shall have due regard to the percentages of loss of earning capacity in relation to different injuries specified in Schedule I;

(*d*) where temporary disablement, whether total or partial, results from the injury
a half-monthly payment of the sum equivalent to twenty-five per cent of monthly wages of the *employee*, to be paid in accordance with the provisions of sub-section (2).

(1A) Notwithstanding anything contained in sub-section (1), while fixing the amount of compensation payable to a *employee* in respect of an accident occurred outside India, the Commissioner shall take into account the amount of compensation, if any, awarded to such *employee* in accordance with the law of the country in which the accident occurred and shall reduce the amount fixed by him by the amount of compensation awarded to the *employee* in accordance with the law of that country.

(1B) The Central Government may, by notification in the Official Gazette, specify, for the purposes of sub-section (1), such monthly wages in relation to an employee as it may consider necessary.

(2) The half-monthly payment referred to in clause (*d*) of sub-section (1) shall be payable on the sixteenth day—

- (*i*) from the date of disablement where such disablement lasts for a period of twenty-eight days or more, or
- (*ii*) after the expiry of a waiting period of three days from the date of disablement where such disablement lasts for a period of less than twenty-eight days; and thereafter half-monthly during the disablement or during a period of five years, whichever period is shorter:

    Provided that—

    - (*a*) there shall be deducted from any lump sum or half-monthly payments to which the *employee* is entitled the amount of any payment or allowance which the *employee* has received from the employer by way of compensation during the period of disablement prior to the receipt of such lump sum or of the first half-monthly payment, as the case may be; and
    - (*b*) no half-monthly payment shall in any case exceed the amount, if any, by which half the amount of the monthly wages of the *employee* before the accident exceeds half the amount of such wages which he is earning after the accident.

Explanation : Any payment or allowance which the *employee* has received from the employer towards his medical treatment shall not be deemed to be a payment or allowance received by him by way of compensation within the meaning of clause (a) of the proviso.

(2A) The employee shall be reimbursed the actual medical expenditure incurred by him for treatment of injuries caused during the course of employment.

(3) On the ceasing of the disablement before the date on which any half-monthly payment falls due, there shall be payable in respect of that half-month a sum proportionate to the duration of the disablement in that half-month.]

(4) If the injury of the *employee* results in his death, the employer shall, in addition to the compensation under sub-section (1), deposit with the Commissioner a sum of *not less than five thousand rupees* for payment of the same to the eldest surviving dependant of the *employee* towards the expenditure of the funeral of such *employee* or where the *employee* did not have a dependant or was not living with his dependant at the time of his death to the person who actually incurred such expenditure.

Provided *that the Central Government may, by notification in the Official Gazette, from time to time, enhance the amount specified in this sub-section.*

Compensation to be paid when due and penalty for default.

4A. (1) Compensation under section 4 shall be paid as soon as it falls due.

(2) In cases where the employer does not accept the liability for compensation to the extent claimed, he shall be bound to make provisional payment based on the extent of liability which he accepts, and, such payment shall be deposited with the Commissioner or made to the *employee*, as the case may be, without prejudice to the right of the *employee* to make any further claim.

(3) Where any employer is in default in paying the compensation due under this Act within one month from the date it fell due, the Commissioner shall—

(*a*) direct that the employer shall, in addition to the amount of the arrears, pay simple interest thereon at the rate of twelve per cent per annum or at such higher rate not exceeding the maximum of the lending rates of any scheduled bank as may be specified by the Central Government, by notification in the Official Gazette, on the amount due; and

(*b*) if, in his opinion, there is no justification for the delay, direct that the employer shall, in addition to the amount of the arrears and interest thereon, pay a further sum not exceeding fifty per cent of such amount by way of penalty :

Provided that an order for the payment of penalty shall not be passed under clause (*b*) without giving a reasonable opportunity to the employer to show cause why it should not be passed.

Explanation: For the purposes of this sub-section, "scheduled bank" means a bank for the time being included in the Second Schedule to the Reserve Bank of India Act, 1934 (2 of 1934).

(3A) The interest and the penalty payable under sub-section (3) shall be paid to the employee or his dependant, as the case may be.

Method of calculating wages.

5. In this Act and for the purposes thereof the expression "monthly wages" means the amount of wages deemed to be payable for a month's service (whether the wages are payable by the month or by whatever other period or at piece rates), and calculated] as follows, namely:—

- (*a*) where the *employee* has, during a continuous period of not less than twelve months immediately preceding the accident, been in the service of the employer who is liable to pay compensation, the monthly wages of the *employee* shall be one-twelfth of the total wages which have fallen due for payment to him by the employer in the last twelve months of that period;

- (*b*) where the whole of the continuous period of service immediately preceding the accident during which the *employee* was in the service of the employer who is liable to pay the compensation was less than one month, the monthly wages of the *employee* shall be the average monthly amount which, during the twelve months immediately preceding the accident, was being earned by a *employee* employed on the same work by the same employer, or, if there was no *employee* so employed, by an *employee* employed on similar work in the same locality;

- (*c*)] in other cases [including cases in which it is not possible for want of necessary information to calculate the monthly wages under clause (*b*), the monthly wages shall be thirty times the total wages earned in respect of the last continuous period of service immediately preceding the accident from the employer who is liable to pay compensation, divided by the number of days comprising such period.

Explanation: A period of service shall, for the purposes of this section be deemed to be continuous which has not been interrupted by a period of absence from work exceeding fourteen days.

Review.

6. (1) Any half-monthly payment payable under this Act, either under an agreement between the parties or under the order of a Commissioner, may be reviewed by the Commissioner, on the application either of the employer or of the *employee* accompanied by the certificate of a qualified medical practitioner that there has been a change in the condition of the *employee* or, subject to rules made under this Act, on application made without such certificate.

(2) Any half-monthly payment may, on review under this section, subject to the provisions of this Act, be continued, increased, decreased or ended, or if the accident is found to have resulted in permanent disablement, be converted to the lump sum to which the *employee* is entitled less any amount which he has already received by way of half-monthly payments.

Commutation of half-monthly payments.

7. Any right to receive half-monthly payments may, by agreement between the parties or, if the parties cannot agree and the payments have been continued for not less than six months, on the application of either party to the Commissioner be redeemed by the payment of a lump sum of such amount as may be agreed to by the parties or determined by the Commissioner, as the case may be.

Distribution of compensation.

8. (1) No payment of compensation in respect of an *employee* whose injury has resulted in death, and no payment of a lump sum as compensation to a woman or a person under a legal disability, shall be made otherwise than by deposit with the Commissioner, and no such payment made directly by an employer shall be deemed to be a payment of compensation:

Provided that, in the case of a deceased *employee*, an employer may make to any dependant advances on account of compensation of an amount equal to three months' wages of such *employee* and so much of such amount as does not exceed the compensation payable to that dependant shall be deducted by the Commissioner from such compensation and repaid to the employer.

(2) Any other sum amounting to not less than ten rupees which is payable as compensation may be deposited with the Commissioner on behalf of the person entitled thereto.

(3) The receipt of the Commissioner shall be a sufficient discharge in respect of any compensation deposited with him.

(4) On the deposit of any money under sub-section (1), as compensation in respect of a deceased *employee* the Commissioner shall, if he thinks necessary, cause notice to be published or to be served on each dependant in such manner as he thinks fit, calling upon the dependants to appear before him on such date as he may fix for determining the distribution of the compensation. If the Commissioner is satisfied after any inquiry which he may deem necessary, that no dependant exists, he shall repay the balance of the money to the employer by whom it was paid. The Commissioner shall, on application by the employer, furnish a statement showing in detail all disbursements made.

(5) Compensation deposited in respect of a deceased *employee* shall, subject to any deduction made under sub-section (4), be apportioned among the dependants of the deceased *employee* or any of them in such proportion as the Commissioner thinks fit, or may, in the discretion of the Commissioner, be allotted to any one dependant.

(6) Where any compensation deposited with the Commissioner is payable to any person, the Commissioner shall, if the person to whom the compensation is payable is not a woman or a person under a legal disability, and may, in other cases, pay the money to the person entitled thereto.

(7) Where any lump sum deposited with the Commissioner is payable to a woman or a person under a legal disability, such sum may be invested, applied or otherwise dealt with for the benefit of the woman, or of such person during his disability, in such manner as the Commissioner may direct; and where a half-monthly payment is payable to any person under a legal disability, the Commissioner may, of his own motion or on an application made to him in this behalf, order that the payment be made during the disability to any dependant of the *employee* or to any other person, whom the Commissioner thinks best fitted to provide for the welfare of the *employee*.

(8) Where, on application made to him in this behalf or otherwise, the Commissioner is satisfied that, on account of neglect of children on the part of a parent or on account of the variation of the circumstances of any dependant or for any other sufficient cause, an order of the Commissioner as to the distribution of any sum paid as compensation or as to the manner in which any sum payable to any such dependant is to be invested, applied or otherwise dealt with, ought to be varied, the Commissioner may make such orders for the variation of the former order as he thinks just in the circumstances of the case:

Provided that no such order prejudicial to any person shall be made unless such person has been given an opportunity of showing cause why the order should not be made, or shall be made in any case in which it would involve the repayment by a dependant of any sum already paid to him.

(9) Where the Commissioner varies any order under sub-section (8) by reason of the fact that payment of compensation to any person has been obtained by fraud, impersonation or other improper means, any amount so paid to or on behalf of such person may be recovered in the manner hereinafter provided in section 31.

Compensation not to be assigned, attached or charged.

9. Save as provided by this Act, no lump sum or half-monthly payment payable under this Act shall in any way be capable of being assigned or charged or be liable to attachment or pass to any person other than the *employee* by operation of law, nor shall any claim be set off against the same.

Notice and claim.

10. (1) No claim for compensation shall be entertained by a Commissioner unless notice of the accident has been given in the manner hereinafter provided as soon as practicable after the happening thereof and unless the claim is preferred before him within two years of the occurrence of the accident or, in case of death, within two years from the date of death:

Provided that, where the accident is the contracting of a disease in respect of which the provisions of sub-section (2) of section 3 are applicable, the accident shall be deemed to have occurred on the first of the days during which the *employee* was continuously absent from work in consequence of the disablement caused by the disease:

Provided further that in case of partial disablement due to the contracting of any such disease and which does not force the *employee* to absent himself from work, the period of two years shall be counted from the day the *employee* gives notice of the disablement to his employer:

Provided further that if a *employee* who, having been employed in an employment for a continuous period, specified under sub-section (2) of section 3 in respect of that employment, ceases to be so employed and develops symptoms of an occupational disease peculiar to that employment within two years of the cessation of employment, the accident shall be deemed to have occurred on the day on which the symptoms were first detected.

Provided further that the want of or any defect or irregularity in a notice shall not be a bar to the entertainment of a claim—

(*a*) if the claim is referred in respect of the death of a *employee* resulting from an accident which occurred on the premises of the employer, or at any place where the *employee* at the time of the accident was working under the control of the employer or of any person employed by him, and the *employee* died on such premises or at such place, or on any premises belonging to the employer, or died without having left the vicinity of the premises or place where the accident occurred, or

(*b*) if the employer or any one of several employers or any person responsible to the employer for the management of any branch of the trade or business in which the injured *employee* was employed] had knowledge of the accident from any other source at or about the time when it occurred:

Provided further that the Commissioner may entertain and decide any claim to compensation in any case notwithstanding that the notice has not been given, or the claim has not been preferred in due time as provided in this sub-section, if he is satisfied that the failure so to give the notice or prefer the claim, as the case may be, was due to sufficient cause.

(2) Every such notice shall give the name and address of the person injured and shall state in ordinary language the cause of the injury and the date on which the accident happened, and shall be served on the employer or upon any one of several employers, or upon any person responsible to the employer for the management of any branch of the trade or business in which the injured *employee* was employed.

(3) The State Government may require that any prescribed class of employers shall maintain at their premises at which *employee* are employed a notice-book, in the prescribed form, which shall be readily accessible at all reasonable times to any injured *employee* employed on the premises and to any person acting *bond fide* on his behalf.

(4) A notice under this section may be served by delivering it at, or sending it by registered post addressed to, the residence or any office or place of business of the person on whom it is to be served, or, where a notice-book is maintained, by entry in the notice book.

Medical examination.

11. (1) Where an *employee* has given notice of an accident, he, shall, if the employer, before the expiry of three days from the time at which service of the notice has been effected, offers to have him examined free of charge by a qualified medical practitioner, submit himself for such examination, and any *employee* who is in receipt of a half-monthly payment under this Act shall, if so required, submit himself for such examination from time to time :

Provided that a *employee* shall not be required to submit himself for examination by a medical practitioner otherwise than in accordance with rules made under this Act, or at more frequent intervals than may be prescribed.

(2) If a *employee*, on being required to do so by the employer under sub-section (1) or by the Commissioner at any time, refuses to submit himself for examination by a qualified medical practitioner or in any way obstructs the same, his right to compensation shall be suspended during the continuance of such refusal or obstruction unless, in the case of refusal, he was prevented by any sufficient cause from so submitting himself.

(3) If a *employee*, before the expiry of the period within which he is liable under sub-section (1) to be required to submit himself for medical examination, voluntarily leaves without having been so examined the vicinity of the place in which he was employed, his right to compensation shall be suspended until he returns and offers himself for such examination.

(4) Where a *employee*, whose right to compensation has been suspended under sub-section (2) or sub-section (3), dies without having submitted himself for medical examination as required by either of those sub-sections, the Commissioner may, if he thinks fit, direct the payment of compensation to the dependants of the deceased *employee*.

(5) Where under sub-section (2) or sub-section (3) a right to compensation is suspended, no compensation shall be payable in respect of the period of suspension, and, if the period of suspension commences before the expiry of the waiting period referred to in clause *(d)* of sub-section (1) of section 4, the waiting period shall be increased by the period during which the suspension continues.

(6) Where an injured *employee* has refused to be attended by a qualified medical practitioner whose services have been offered to him by the employer free of charge or having accepted such offer has deliberately disregarded the instructions of such medical practitioner, then, if it is proved that the *employee* has not thereafter been regularly attended by a qualified medical practitioner or having been so attended has deliberately failed to follow his instructions and that such refusal, disregard or failure was unreasonable] in the circumstances of the case and that the injury has been aggravated thereby, the injury and resulting disablement shall be deemed to be of the same nature and duration as they might reasonably have been expected to be if the *employee* had been regularly attended by a qualified medical practitioner, whose instructions he had followed, and compensation, if any, shall be payable accordingly.

Contracting.

12. (1) Where any person (hereinafter in this section referred to as the principal) in the course of or for the purposes of his trade or business contracts with any other person (hereinafter in this section referred to as the contractor) for the execution by or under the contractor of the whole or any part of any work which is ordinarily part of the trade or business of the principal, the principal shall be liable to pay to any *employee* employed in the execution of the work any compensation which he would have been liable to pay if that *employee* had been immediately employed by him; and where compensation is claimed from the principal, this Act shall apply as if references to the principal were substituted for references to the employer except that the amount of compensation shall be calculated with reference to the wages of the *employee* under the employer by whom he is immediately employed.

(2) Where the principal is liable to pay compensation under this section, he shall be entitled to be indemnified by the contractor, or any other person from whom the *employee* could have recovered compensation and where a contractor who is himself a principal is liable to pay compensation or to indemnify a principal under this section he shall be entitled to be indemnified by any person standing to him in the relation of a contractor from whom the *employee* could have recovered compensation,] and all questions as to the right to and the amount of any such indemnity shall, in default of agreement, be settled by the Commissioner.

(3) Nothing in this section shall be construed as preventing a *employee* from recovering compensation from the contractor instead of the principal.

(4) This section shall not apply in any case where the accident occurred elsewhere than on, in or about the premises on which the principal has undertaken or usually undertakes, as the case may be, to execute the work or which are otherwise under his control or management.

Remedies of employer against stranger.

13. Where an *employee* has recovered compensation in respect of any injury caused under circumstances creating a legal liability of some person other than the person by whom the compensation was paid to pay damages in respect thereof, the person by whom the compensation was paid and any person who has been called on to pay an indemnity under section 12 shall be entitled to be indemnified by the person so liable to pay damages as aforesaid.

Insolvency of employer.

14. (1) Where any employer has entered into a contract with any insurers in respect of any liability under this Act to any *employee*, then in the event of the employer becoming insolvent or making a composition or scheme of arrangement with his creditors or, if the employer is a company, in the event of the company having commenced to be wound up, the rights of the employer against the insurers as respects that liability shall, notwithstanding anything in any law for the time being in force relating to insolvency or the winding up of companies, be transferred to and vest in the *employee*, and upon any such transfer the insurers shall have the same rights and remedies and be subject to the same liabilities as if they were the employer, so, however, that the insurers shall not be under any greater liability to the *employee* than they would have been under to the employer.

(2) If the liability of the insurers to the *employee* is less than the liability of the employer to the *employee*, the *employee* may prove for the balance in the insolvency proceedings or liquidation.

(3) Where in any case such as is referred to in sub-section(1) the contract of the employer with the insurers is void or voidable by reason of non-compliance on the part of the employer with any terms or conditions of the contract (other than a stipulation for the payment of premia), the provisions of that sub-section shall apply as if the contract were not void or voidable, and the insurers shall be entitled to prove in the insolvency proceedings or liquidation for the amount paid to the *employee* :

Provided that the provisions of this sub-section shall not apply in any case in which the *employee* fails to give notice to the insurers of the happening of the accident and of any resulting disablement as soon as practicable after he becomes aware of the institution of the insolvency or liquidation proceedings.

(4) There shall be deemed to be included among the debts which under section 49 of the Presidency-towns Insolvency Act, 1909 (3 of 1909), or under section 61 of the Provincial Insolvency Act, 1920 (5 of 1920), or under section 530 of the Companies Act, 1956 (1 of 1956), are in the distribution of the property of an insolvent or in the distribution of the assets of a company being wound up to be paid in priority to all other debts, the amount due in respect of any compensation the liability wherefor accrued before the date of the order of adjudication of the insolvent or the date of the commencement of the winding up, as the case may be, and those Acts shall have effect accordingly.

(5) Where the compensation is a half-monthly payment, the amount due in respect thereof shall, for the purposes of this section, be taken to be the amount of the lump sum for which the half-monthly payment could, if redeemable, be redeemed if application were made for that purpose under section 7, and a certificate of the Commissioner as to the amount of such sum shall be conclusive proof thereof.

(6) The provisions of sub-section (4) shall apply in the case of any amount for which an insurer is entitled to prove under sub-section (3), but otherwise those provisions shall not apply where the insolvent or the company being wound up has entered into such a contract with insurers as is referred to in sub-section (1).

(7) This section shall not apply where a company is wound up voluntarily merely for to purposes of reconstruction or of amalgamation with another company.

Special provisions relating to masters and seamen.

15. This Act shall apply in the case of *employees* who are masters of ships or seamen subject to the following modifications, namely :—

(1) The notice of the accident and the claim for compensation may, except where the person injured is the master of the ship, be served on the master of the ship as if he were the employer, but where the accident happened and the disablement commenced on board the ship, it shall not be necessary for any seaman to give any notice of the accident.

(2) In the case of the death of a master or seaman, the claim for compensation shall be made within one year after the news of the death has been received by the claimant or, where the ship has been or is deemed to have been lost with all hands, within eighteen months of the date on which the ship was, or is deemed to have been, so lost.

Provided that the Commissioner may entertain any claim to compensation in any case notwithstanding that the claim has not been preferred in due time as provided in this sub-section, if he is satisfied that the failure so to prefer the claim was due to sufficient cause.

(3) Where an injured master or seaman is discharged or left behind in any part of India or in any foreign country any depositions taken by any Judge or Magistrate in that part or by any Consular Officer in the foreign country and transmitted by the person by whom they are taken to the Central Government or any State Government shall, in any proceedings for enforcing the claim, be admissible in evidence :

(*a*) if the deposition is authenticated by the signature of the Judge, Magistrate or Consular Officer before whom it is made;

(*b*) if the defendant or the person accused, as the case may be, had an opportunity by himself or his agent to cross-examine the witness; and

(*c*) if the deposition was made in the course of a criminal proceeding, on proof that the deposition was made in the presence of the person accused;

and it shall not be necessary in any case to prove the signature or official character of the person appearing to have signed any such deposition and a certificate by such person that the defendant or the person accused had an opportunity of cross-examining the witness and that the deposition if made in a criminal proceeding was made in the presence of the person accused shall, unless the contrary is proved, be sufficient evidence that he had that opportunity and that it was so made.

(4) No half-monthly payment shall be payable in respect of the period during which the owner of the ship is, under any law in force for the time being relating to merchant shipping, liable to defray the expenses of maintenance of the injured master or seaman.

(5) No compensation shall be payable under this Act in respect of any injury in respect of which provision is made for payment of a gratuity, allowance or pension under the War Pensions and Detention Allowances (Mercantile Marine, etc.) Scheme, 1939, or the War Pensions and Detention Allowances (Indian Seamen, etc.) Scheme, 1941, made under the Pensions (Navy, Army, Air Force and Mercantile Marine) Act, 1939, or under War pensions and Detention Allowances (Indian Seaman) Scheme, 1942, made by the Central Government.

(6) Failure to give a notice or make a claim or commence proceedings within the time required by this Act shall not be a bar to the maintenance of proceedings under this Act in respect of any personal injury, if—

(*a*) an application has been made for payment in respect of the injury under any of the schemes referred to in the preceding clause, and

(*b*) the State Government certifies that the said application was made in the reasonable belief that the injury was one in respect of which the scheme under which the application was made makes provision for payments, and that the application was rejected or that payments made in pursuance of the application were discontinued on the ground that the injury was not such an injury, and

(*c*) the proceedings under this Act are commenced within one month from the date on which the said certificate of the State Government was furnished to the person commencing the proceedings.

Returns as to compensation.

16. The State Government may, by notification in the Official Gazette, direct that every person employing *employees*, or that any specified class of such persons, shall send at such time and in such form and to such authority, as may be specified in the notification, a correct return specifying the number of injuries in respect of which compensation has been paid by the employer during the previous year and the amount of such compensation together with such other particulars as to the compensation as the State Government may direct.

Contracting out.

17. Any contract or agreement whether made before or after the commencement of this Act, whereby an *employee* relinquishes any right of compensation from the employer for personal injury arising out of or in the course of the employment, shall be null and void in so far as it purports to remove or reduce the liability of any person to pay compensation under this Act.

Proof of age

18. [*Omitted by the Workmen's Compensation (Amendment) Act, 1959, w.e.f. 1-6-1959.*]

CHAPTER III

COMMISSIONERS

Reference to Commissioners.

19. (1) If any question arises in any proceedings under this Act as to the liability of any person to pay compensation (including any question as to whether a person injured is or is not an *employee*) or as to the amount or duration of compensation (including any question as to the nature or extent of disablement), the question shall, in default of agreement, be settled by a Commissioner.

(2) No Civil Court shall have jurisdiction to settle, decide or deal with any question which is by or under this Act required to be settled, decided or dealt with by a Commissioner or to enforce any liability incurred under this Act.

Appointment of Commissioner.

20. (1) The State Government may, by notification in the Official Gazette, appoint any person *who is or has been a member of a State Judicial Service for a period of not less than five years or is or has been for not less than five years an advocate or a pleader or is or has been a Gazetted Officer for not less than five years having educational qualifications and experience in personnel management, human resource development and industrial relations* to be a Commissioner for *employees'* Compensation for such area as may be specified in the notification.

(2) Where more than one Commissioner has been appointed for any area, the State Government may, by general or special order, regulate the distribution of business between them.

(3)] Any Commissioner may, for the purpose of deciding any matter referred to him for decision under this Act, choose one or more persons possessing special knowledge of any matter relevant to the matter under inquiry to assist him in holding the inquiry.

(4)] Every Commissioner shall be deemed to be a public servant within the meaning of the Indian Penal Code (45 of 1860).

Venue of proceedings and transfer.

21. (1) Where any matter under this Act is to be done by or before a Commissioner, the same shall, subject to the provisions of this Act and to any rules made hereunder, be done by or before the Commissioner for the area in which—

- (a) the accident took place which resulted in the injury; or
- (b) the *employee* or in case of his death, the dependant claiming the compensation ordinarily resides; or
- (c) the employer has his registered office :

Provided that no matter shall be processed before or by a Commissioner, other than the Commissioner having jurisdiction over the area in which the accident took place, without his giving notice in the manner prescribed by the Central Government to the Commissioner having jurisdiction over the area and the State Government concerned :

Provided further that, where the *employee*, being the master of a ship or a seaman or the captain or a member of the crew of an aircraft or an *employee* in a motor vehicle or a company, meets with the accident outside India any such matter may be done by or before a Commissioner for the area in which the owner or agent of the ship, aircraft or motor vehicle resides or carries on business or the registered office of the company is situate, as the case may be.

(1A) If a Commissioner, other than the Commissioner with whom any money has been deposited under section 8, proceeds with a matter under this Act, the former may for the proper disposal of the matter call for transfer of any records or money remaining with the latter and on receipt of such a request, he shall comply with the same.

(2) If a Commissioner is satisfied that any matter arising out of any proceedings pending before him can be more conveniently dealt with by any other Commissioner, whether in the same State or not, he may, subject to rules made under this Act, order such matter to be transferred to such other Commissioner either for report or for disposal, and, if he does so, shall forthwith transmit to such other Commissioner all documents relevant for the decision of such matter and, where the matter is transferred for disposal, shall also transmit in the prescribed manner any money remaining in his hands or invested by him for the benefit of any party to the proceedings:

Provided that the Commissioner shall not, where any party to the proceedings has appeared before him, make any order of transfer relating to the distribution among dependants of a lump sum without giving such party an opportunity of being heard.

(3) The Commissioner to whom any matter is so transferred shall, subject to rules made under this Act, inquire thereinto and, if the matter was transferred for report, return his report thereon or, if the matter was transferred for disposal, continue the proceedings as if they had originally commenced before him.

(4) On receipt of a report from a Commissioner to whom any matter has been transferred for report under sub-section (2), the Commissioner by whom it was referred shall decide the matter referred in conformity with such report.

(5) The State Government may transfer any matter from any Commissioner appointed by it to any other Commissioner appointed by it.

Form of application.

22. (1) Where an accident occurs in respect of which liability to pay compensation under this Act arises, a claim for such compensation may, subject to the provisions of this Act, be made before the Commissioner.

(1A) Subject to the provisions of sub-section (1), no application for the settlement of any matter by a Commissioner, other than an application by a dependant or dependants for compensation shall be made unless and until some question has arisen between the parties in connection therewith which they have been unable to settle by agreement.

(2) An application to a Commissioner may be made in such form and shall be accompanied by such fee, if any, as may be prescribed, and shall contain, in addition to any particulars which may be prescribed, the following particulars, namely:—

- (*a*) a concise statement of the circumstances in which the application is made and the relief or order which the applicant claims;
- (*b*) in the case of a claim for compensation against an employer, the date of service of notice of the accident on the employer and, if such notice has not been served or has not been served in due time, the reason for such omission;
- (*c*) the names and addresses of the parties ; and
- (*d*) except in the case of an application by dependants for compensation a concise statement of the matters on which agreement has and of those on which agreement has not been come to.

(3) If the applicant is illiterate or for any other reason is unable to furnish the required information in writing, the application shall, if the applicant so desires, be prepared under the direction of the Commissioner.

Powers and procedure of Commissioners.

23. The Commissioner shall have all the powers of a Civil Court under the Code of Civil Procedure, 1908 (5 of 1908) for the purpose of taking evidence on oath (which such Commissioner is hereby empowered to impose) and of enforcing the attendance of witnesses and compelling the production of documents and material objects and the Commissioner shall be deemed to be a Civil Court for all the purposes of section 195 and of Chapter XXVI of the Code of Criminal Procedure, 1973 (2 of 1974).

Appearance of parties.

24. Any appearance, application or act required to be made or done by any person before or to a Commissioner (other than an appearance of a party which is required for the purpose of his examination as a witness) may be made or done on behalf of such person by a legal practitioner or by an official of an Insurance Company or registered trade union] or by an Inspector appointed under sub-section (1) of section 8 of the Factories Act, 1948 (63 of 1948), or under sub-section (1) of section 5 of the Mines Act, 1952, (35 of 1952), or by any other officer specified by the State Government in this behalf, authorised in writing by such person, or, with the permission of the Commissioner, by any other person so authorised.

Method of recording evidence.

25. The Commissioner shall make a brief memorandum of the substance of the evidence of every witness as the examination of the witness proceeds, and such memorandum shall be written and signed by the Commissioner with his own hand and shall form part of the record:

Provided that, if the Commissioner is prevented from making such memorandum, he shall record the reason of his inability to do so and shall cause such memorandum to be made in writing from his dictation and shall sign the same, and such memorandum shall form a part of the record:

Provided further that the evidence of any medical witness shall be taken down as nearby as may be word for word.

Time limit for disposal of cases relating to compensation.

25A. *The Commissioner shall dispose of the matter relating to compensation under this Act within a period of three months from the date of reference and intimate the decision in respect thereof within the said period to the employee.*

Costs.

26. All costs, incidental to any proceedings before a Commissioner, shall, subject to rules made under this Act, be in the discretion of the Commissioner.

Power to submit cases.

27. A Commissioner may, if he thinks fit, submit any question of law for the decision of the High Court and, if he does so, shall decide the question in conformity with such decision.

Registration of agreements.

28. (1) Where the amount of any lump sum payable as compensation has been settled by agreement, whether by way of redemption of a half-monthly payment or otherwise, or where any compensation has been so settled as being payable to a woman or a person under a legal disability a memorandum thereof shall be sent by the employer to the Commissioner, who shall, on being satisfied as to its genuineness, record the memorandum in a register in the prescribed manner:

Provided that—

(*a*) no such memorandum shall be recorded before seven days after communication by the Commissioner of notice to the parties concerned;

* * *

(*c*) the Commissioner may at any time rectify the register;

(*d*) where it appears to the Commissioner that an agreement as to the payment of a lump sum whether by way of redemption of a half-monthly payment or otherwise, or an agreement as to the amount of compensation payable to a woman or a person under a legal disability ought not to be registered by reason of the inadequacy of the sum or amount, or by reason of the agreement having been obtained by fraud or undue influence or other improper means, he may refuse to record the memorandum of the agreement and may make such order including an order as to any sum already paid under the agreement, as he thinks just in the circumstances.

(2) An agreement for the payment of compensation which has been registered under sub-section (1) shall be enforceable under this Act notwithstanding anything contained in the Indian Contract Act, 1872 (9 of 1872), or in any other law for the time being in force.

Effect of failure to register agreement.

29. Where a memorandum of any agreement, the registration of which is required by section 28, is not sent to the Commissioner as required by that section, the employer shall be liable to pay the full amount of compensation which he is liable to pay under the provisions of this Act, and notwithstanding anything contained in the proviso to sub-section (1) of section 4, shall not, unless the Commissioner otherwise directs, be entitled to deduct more than half of any amount paid to the *employees* by way of compensation whether under the agreement or otherwise.

Appeals

30. (1) An appeal shall lie to the High Court from the following orders of a Commissioner, namely:—

(*a*) an order awarding as compensation a lump sum whether by way of redemption of a half-monthly payment or otherwise or disallowing a claim in full or in part for a lump sum;

(*aa*) an order awarding interest or penalty under section 4A;

(*b*) an order refusing to allow redemption of a half-monthly payment;

(*c*) an order providing for the distribution of compensation among the dependants of a deceased *employee*, or disallowing any claim of a person alleging himself to be such dependant;

(*d*) an order allowing or disallowing any claim for the amount of an indemnity under the provisions of sub-section (2) of section 12; or

(*e*) an order refusing to register a memorandum of agreement or registering the same or providing for the registration of the same subject to conditions:

Provided that no appeal shall lie against any order unless a substantial question of law is involved in the appeal and, in the case of an order other than an order such as is referred to in clause (*b*) unless the amount in dispute in the appeal is not less than three hundred rupees:

Provided further that no appeal shall lie in any case in which the parties have agreed to abide by the decision of the Commissioner, or in which the order of the Commissioner gives effect to an agreement come to by the parties.

Provided further that no appeal by an employer under clause (*a*) shall lie unless the memorandum of appeal is accompanied by a certificate by the Commissioner to the effect that the appellant has deposited with him the amount payable under the order appealed against.]

(2) The period of limitation for an appeal under this section shall be sixty days.

(3) The provision of section 5 of the Limitation Act, 1963 (36 of 1963) shall be applicable to appeals under this section.

Recovery.

31. The Commissioner may recover as an arrear of land revenue any amount payable by any person under this Act, whether under an agreement for the payment of compensation or otherwise, and the Commissioner shall be deemed to be a public officer within the meaning of section 5 of the Revenue Recovery Act, 1890 (1 of 1890).

CHAPTER IV
RULES

Power of the State Government to make rules.

32. (1) The State Government may make rules to carry out the purposes of this Act.

(2) In particular and without prejudice to the generality of the foregoing power, such rules may provide for all or any of the following matters, namely:—

(*a*) for prescribing the intervals at which and the conditions subject to which an application for review may be made under section 6 when not accompanied by a medical certificate;

(*b*) for prescribing the intervals at which and the conditions subject to which an *employee* may be required to submit himself for medical examination under sub-section (1) of section 11;

(*c*) for prescribing the procedure to be followed by Commissioners in the disposal of cases under this Act and by the parties in such cases;

(*d*) for regulating the transfer of matters and cases from one Commissioner to another and the transfer of money in such cases;

(e) for prescribing the manner in which money in the hands of a Commissioner may be invested for the benefit of dependants of a deceased *employee* and for the transfer of money so invested from one Commissioner to another;

(f) for the representation in proceedings before Commissioners of parties who are minors or are unable to make an appearance;

(g) for prescribing the form and manner in which memoranda of agreements shall be presented and registered;

(h) for the withholding by Commissioners, whether in whole or in part of half-monthly payments pending decision on applications for review of the same;

(i) for regulating the scales of costs which may be allowed in proceedings under this Act;

(j) for prescribing and determining the amount of the fees payable in respect of any proceedings before a Commissioner under this Act;

(k) for the maintenance by Commissioners of registers and records of proceedings before them;

(l) for-prescribing the classes of employers who shall maintain notice-books under sub-section (3) of section 10, and the form of such notice-books;

(m) for prescribing the form of statement to be submitted by employers under section 10A;

(n) for prescribing the cases in which the report referred to in section 10B may be sent to an authority other than the Commissioner;

(o) for prescribing abstracts of this Act and requiring the employers to display notices containing such abstracts;

(p) for prescribing the manner in which diseases specified as occupational diseases may be diagnosed;

(q) for prescribing the manner in which diseases may be certified for any of the purposes of this Act;

(r) for prescribing the manner in which, and the standards by which, incapacity may be assessed.

(3) Every rule made under this section shall be laid, as soon as may be after it is made, before the State Legislature.

Power of Local Government to make rules

33. [* * *]

Publication of rules

34. (1) The power to make rules conferred by section 32 shall be subject to the condition of the rules being made after previous publication.

(2) The date to be specified in accordance with clause (3) of section 23 of the General Clauses Act, 1897 (10 of 1897), as that after which a draft of rules proposed to be made under section 32 will be taken into consideration, shall not be less than three months from the date on which the draft of the proposed rules was published for general information.

(3) Rules so made shall be published in the Official Gazette and, on such publication, shall have effect as if enacted in this Act.

Rules to give effect to arrangements with other countries for the transfer of money paid as compensation.

35. (1)] The Central Government may, by notification in the Official Gazette, make rules for the transfer to any foreign country of money deposited with a Commissioner under this Act which has been awarded to or may be due to, any person residing or about to reside in such foreign country and for the receipt, distribution and administration in any State of any money deposited under the law relating to *employees'* compensation in any foreign, country, which has been awarded to, or may be due to any person residing or about to reside in any State.:

Provided that no sum deposited under this Act in respect of fatal accidents shall be so transferred without the consent of the employer concerned until the Commissioner receiving the sum has passed orders determining its distribution and apportionment under the provisions of sub-sections (4) and (5) of section 8.

(2) Where money deposited with a Commissioner has been so transferred in accordance with the rules made under this section, the provisions elsewhere contained in this Act regarding distribution by the Commissioner of compensation deposited with him shall cease to apply in respect of any such money.

Rules made by Central Government to be laid before Parliament.

36. Every rule made under this Act by the Central Government shall be laid as soon as may be after it is made before each House of Parliament while it is in session for a total period of thirty days which may be comprised in one session or in two or more successive sessions, and if, before the expiry of the session immediately following the session or the successive sessions aforesaid, both Houses agree in making any modification in the rule or both Houses agree that the rule should not be made, the rule shall thereafter have effect only in such modified form or be of no effect, as the case may be; so however that any such modification or annulment shall be without prejudice to the validity of anything previously done under that rule.

SCHEDULE I

[*See* sections 2(1) and (4)]

PART I

LIST OF INJURIES DEEMED TO RESULT IN PERMANENT TOTAL DISABLEMENT

Serial No.	Description of injury	Percentage of loss of earning capacity
1	2	3
1.	Loss of both hands or amputation at higher sites	100
2.	Loss of a hand and foot	100
3.	Double amputation through leg or thigh, or amputation through leg or thigh on one side and loss of other foot	100
4.	Loss of sight to such an extent as to render the claimant unable to perform any work for which eye sight is essential.	100
5.	Very severe facial disfigurement	100
6.	Absolute deafness	100

PART II

LIST OF INJURIES DEEMED TO RESULT IN PERMANENT PARTIAL DISABLEMENT]

Amputation Cases - Upper limbs - Either arm

[1]	Amputation through shoulder joint	90
[2]	Amputation below shoulder with stump less than 20.32 cms. from tip of acromion	80
[3]	Amputation from 20.32 cms. from tip of acromion to less than 4" below tip of olecranon	70
[4]	Loss of a hand or of the thumb and four fingers of one hand or	60

		amputation from 11.43 cms. below tip of olecranon	
[5]	Loss of thumb		30
[6]	Loss of thumb and its metacarpal bone		40
[7]	Loss of four fingers of one hand		50
[8]	Loss of three fingers of one hand		30
[9]	Loss of two fingers of one hand		20
[10]	Loss of terminal phalanx of thumb		20
[10A	Guillotine amputation of tip of thumb without loss of bone.		10]

	Amputation cases - lower limbs	
[11]	Amputation of both feet resulting in end-bearing stumps.	90
[12]	Amputation through both feet proximal to the metatarso-phalangeal joint	80
[13]	Loss of all toes of both feet through the metatarso-phalangeal joint	40
[14]	Loss of all toes of both feet proximal to the proximal inter-phalangeal joint	30
[15]	Loss of all toes of both feet distal to the proximal inter-phalangeal joint	20
[16]	Amputation at hip	90
[17]	Amputation below hip with stump not exceeding 12.70 cms. in length measured from; tip of great trenchanter	80
[18]	Amputation below hip with stump exceeding 12.70 cms. in length measured from tip of great trenchanter but not beyond middle thigh	70
[19]	Amputation below middle thigh to 8.89 cms. below knee	60
[20]	Amputation below knee with stump exceeding 8.89 cms. but not exceeding 12.70 cms.	50

[21]	Amputation below knee with stump exceeding 12.70 cms.		50
[22]	Amputation of one foot resulting in end-bearing		50
[23]	Amputation through one foot proximal to the metatarso-phalangeal joint		50
[24]	Loss of all toes of one foot through the metatarso-phalangeal joint		20
	Other injuries		
[25]	Loss of one eye, without complications, the other being normal		40
[26]	Loss of vision of one eye. without complications or disfigurement of eye-ball, the other being normal		30
[26A.	Loss of partial vision of one eye		10
	Loss of - A. Fingers of right or left hand Index finger		
[27]	Whole		14
[28]	Two phalanges		11
[29]	One phalanx		9
[30]	Guillotine amputation of tip without loss of bone		5
	Middle finger		
[31]	Whole		12
[32]	Two phalanges		9
[33]	One phalanx		7
[34]	Guillotine amputation of tip without loss of bone		4
	Ring or little finger		

[35]	Whole	7
[36]	Two phalanges	6
[37]	One phalanx	5
[38]	Guillotine amputation of tip without loss of bone	2
	B. Toes of right or left foot great toe	
[39]	Through metatarso-phalangeal joint	14
[40]	Part, with some loss of bone	3
	Any other toe	
[41]	Through metatarso-phalangeal joint	3
[42]	Part, with some loss of bone	1
	Two toes of one foot, excluding great toe	
[43]	Through metatarso-phalangeal joint	5
[44]	Part, with some loss of bone	2
	Three toes of one foot, excluding great toe	
[45]	Through metatarso-phalangeal joint	6
[46]	Part, with some loss of bone	6
	Four toes of one foot, excluding great toe	

| [47] | Through metatarso-phalangeal joint | 9 |
| [48] | Part, with some loss of bone | 3 |

Note - Complete and permanent loss of the use of any limb or member referred to in this Schedule shall be deemed to be equivalent to the loss of that limb or member.

SCHEDULE II

[See section 2(l)(dd)]

LIST OF PERSONS WHO SUBJECT TO THE PROVISIONS OF SECTION 2(1)(n), ARE INCLUDED IN THE DEFINITION OF WORKMEN

The following persons are *employees* within the meaning of *section 2(l)(dd)* and subject to the provisions of that section, that is to say, any person who is—

(*i*) *employed in railways*, otherwise than in a clerical capacity or on a railway, in connection with the operation repair or maintenance of a lift or a vehicle propelled by steam or other mechanical power or by electricity or in connection with the loading or unloading of any such vehicle; or

(*ii*) employed, in any premises wherein or within the precincts whereof a manufacturing process as defined in clause *(k)* of section 2 of the Factories Act, 1948 (63 of 1948), is being carried on, or in any kind of work whatsoever incidental to or connected with any such manufacturing process or with the article made, whether or not employment in any such work is within such premises or precincts and steam, water or other mechanical power or electrical power is used; or

(*iii*) employed for the purpose of making, altering, repairing, ornamenting, finishing or otherwise adapting for use, transport or sale of any article or part of an article in any premises.

Explanation: For the purposes of this clause, persons employed outside such premises or precincts but in any work incidental to, or connected with, the work relating to making, altering, repairing, ornamenting, finishing or otherwise adapting for use, transport or sale of any articles or part of an article shall be deemed to be employed within such premises or precincts; or

(*iv*) employed in the manufacture or handling of explosives in connection with the employer's trade or business; or

(*v*) employed, in any mine as defined in clause (j) of section 2 of the Mines Act, 1952 (35 of 1952), in any mining operation or in any kind of work, incidental to or connected with any mining operation or with the mineral obtained, or in any kind of work whatsoever below ground; or

(*vi*) employed as the master or as a seaman of—

(*a*) any ship which is propelled wholly or in part by steam or other mechanical power or by electricity or which is towed or intended to be towed by a ship so propelled; or

(*b*) [***]

(*c*) any sea-going ship not included in sub-clause (a) provided with sufficient area for navigation under sails alone; or

(*vii*) employed for the purpose of—

(*a*) loading, unloading, fuelling, constructing, repairing, demolishing, cleaning or painting any ship of which he is not the master or a member of the crew, or handling or transport within the limits of any port subject to the Ports Act, 1908 (15 of 1908) or the Major Port Trusts Act, 1963 (38 of 1963)], of goods which have been discharged from or are to be loaded into any vessel; or

(*b*) warping a ship through the lock; or

(*c*) mooring and unmooringships at harbour wall berths t)r in pier; or

(*d*) removing or replacing dry dock caisoons when vessels are entering or leaving dry docks; or

(*e*) the docking or undocking or any vessel during an emergency; or

(*f*) preparing splicing coir springs and check wires, painting depth marks on lock-sides, removing or replacing fenders whenever necessary, landing of gangways, maintaining life-buoys up to standard or any other maintenance work of a like nature; or

(*g*) any work on jolly-boats for bringing a ship's line to the wharf; or (*viii*) employed in the construction, maintenance, repair or demolition of—

(*a*) any building which is designed to be or is or has been more than one storey in height above the ground or twelve feet or more from the ground level to the apex of the roof; or

(*b*) any dam or embankment which is twelve feet or more in height from its lowest to its highest point; or

(*c*) any road, bridge, tunnel or canal; or

(*d*) any wharf, quay, sea-wall or other marine work including any moorings of ships; or

(*ix*) employed in setting up, maintaining, repairing or taking down any telegraph or telephone line or post or any overhead electric line or cable or post or standard or fittings and fixtures for the same; or]

(*x*) employed, in the construction, working, repair or demolition of any aerial ropeway, canal, pipeline, or sewer; or

(*xi*) employed in the service of any fire brigade; or

(*xii*) employed upon a railway as defined in clause (*31*) of section 2 and sub-section (1) of section 197 of the Railways Act, 1989 (24 of 1989), either directly or through a sub-contractor, by a person fulfilling a contract with the railway administration; or

(*xiii*) employed as an inspector, mail guard, sorter or van peon in the Railway Mail Service, or as a telegraphist or as a postal or railway signaller or employed in any occupation ordinarily involving outdoor work in the Indian Posts and Telegraphs Department; or

(*xiv*) employed, in connection with operations for winning natural petroleum or natural gas; or

(*xv*) employed in any occupation involving blasting operations; or

(*xvi*) employed in the making of any excavation or explosives have been used, or whose depth from its highest to its lowest point exceeds twelve feet; or

(*xvii*) employed in the operation of any ferry boat capable of carrying more than ten persons; or

(*xviii*) *employed on any estate which is maintained for the purpose of growing cardamom, cinchona, coffee, rubber or tea;* or

(*xix*) employed, in the generating, transforming, transmitting or distribution of electrical energy or in generation or supply of gas; or (*xx*) employed in a lighthouse as defined in clause (d) of section 2 of the Indian Lighthouse Act, 1927 (17 of 1927); or

(*xxi*) employed in producing cinematograph pictures intended for public exhibition or in exhibiting such pictures; or

(*xxii*) employed in the training, keeping or working of elephants or wild animals; or

(*xxiii*) employed in the tapping of palm-trees or the felling or logging of trees, or the transport of timber by inland waters, or the control or extinguishing of forest fires; or

(*xxiv*) employed in operations for the catching or hunting of elephants or other wild animals; or

(*xxv*)] employed as a driver ; or

(*xxvi*) employed in the handling or transport of goods in, or within the precincts of,—

(*a*) any warehouse or other place in which goods are stored, or

(*b*) any market; or

(*xxvii*) employed in any occupation involving the handling and manipulation of radium or X-rays apparatus, or contact with radio-active substances or

(*xxviii*) employed in or in connection with the construction, erection, dismantling, operation or maintenance of an aircraft as defined in section 2 of the Indian Aircraft Act, 1934 (22 of 1934); or

(*xxix*) employed in horticultural operations, forestry, bee-keeping or farming by tractors or other contrivances driven by steam or other mechanical power or by electricity; or

(*xxx*) employed, in the construction, working, repair or maintenance of a tube well; or

(*xxxi*) employed in the maintenance, repair or renewal of electric fittings in any building; or

(*xxxii*) employed in a circus.]

(*xxxiii*) employed as watchman in any factory or establishment; or

(*xxxiv*) employed in any operation in the sea for catching fish; or

(*xxxv*) employed in any employment which requires handling of snakes for the purpose of extraction of venom or for the purpose of looking after snakes or handling any other poisonous animal or insect; or

(*xxxvi*) employed in handling animals like horses, mules and bulls; or

(*xxxvii*) employed for the purpose of loading or unloading any mechanically propelled vehicle or in the handling or transport of goods which have been loaded in such vehicles; or (*xxxviii*) employed in cleaning of sewer lines or septic tanks within the limits of a local authority; or

(*xxxix*) employed on surveys and investigation, exploration or gauge or discharge observation of rivers including drilling operations, hydro-logical observations and flood forecasting activities ground, water surveys and exploration; or

(*xl*) employed in cleaning of jungles or reclaiming land or ponds; or

(*xli*) employed in cultivation of land or rearing and maintenance of livestock or forest operations or fishing; or

(*xlii*) employed in installation, maintenance or repair of pumping equipment used for lifting of water from wells, tubewells, ponds, lakes, streams and the like; or

(*xliii*) employed in the construction, boring or deepening of an open well or dug well, bore well, bore-cum-dug well, filter-point and the like; or

(*xliv*) employed in spraying and dusting of insecticides or pesticides in agricultural operations or plantations; or

(*xlv*) employed in mechanised harvesting and threshing operations; or

(*xlvi*) employed in working or repair or maintenance of bulldozers, tractors, power tillers and the like; or

(*xlvii*) employed as artist for drawing pictures on advertisement boards at a height of 3.66 metres or more from the ground level; or

(*xlviii*) employed in any newspaper establishment as defined in the Working Journalists and other Newspaper Employees (Conditions of Service) and Miscellaneous Provisions Act, 1955 (45 of 1955) and engaged in outdoor work;]

(*xlix*) employed as divers for work under water.]

Explanation.— [***]

SCHEDULE III

(See section 3)

LIST OF OCCUPATIONAL DISEASES

S. No.	Occupational disease	Employment
(1)	*(2)*	*(3)*
	PART A	
1.	Infectious and parasitic diseases contracted in an occupation where there is a particular risk of contamination.	(*a*) All work involving exposure to health or laboratory work;
		(*b*) All work involving exposure to veterinary work;
		(*c*) Work relating to handling animals, animal carcasses, part of such carcasses, or merchandise which may have been contaminated by animals or animal carcasses;
		(*d*) Other work carrying a particular risk of contamination.
2.	Diseases caused "by work in compressed air.	All work involving exposure to the risk concerned.
3.	Diseases caused by lead or its toxic compounds.	All work involving exposure to the risk concerned.
4.	Poisoning by nitrous fumes.	All work involving exposure to the risk concerned.
5.	Poisoning by organo phosphorus compounds.	All work involving exposure to the risk concerned.
	PART B	
1.	Diseases caused by phosphorus or its toxic compounds.	All work involving exposure to the risk concerned.
2.	Diseases caused by mercury or its toxic	All work involving exposure to

	compounds.	the risk concerned.
3.	Diseases caused by benzene or its toxic homologues.	All work involving exposure to the risk concerned.
4.	Diseases caused by nitro and amido toxic derivatives of benzene or its homologues.	All work involving exposure to the risk concerned.
5.	Diseases caused by chromium or its toxic compounds.	All work involving exposure to the risk concerned.
6.	Diseases caused by arsenic or its toxic compounds.	All work involving exposure to the risk concerned.
7.	Diseases caused by radioactive substances and ionising radiations.	All work involving exposure to the action of radioactive substances or ionising radiations.
8.	Primary epitheliomatous cancer of the skin caused by tar, pitch, bitumen, mineral oil, anthracene, or the compounds, products or residues of these substances.	All work involving exposure to the risk concerned.
9.	Disease caused by the toxic halogen derivatives of hydrocarbons (of the aliphatic and aromatic series)	All work involving exposure to the risk concerned.
10.	Diseases caused by carbon disulphide.	All work involving exposure to the risk concerned.
11.	Occupational cataract due to infra-red radiations.	All work involving exposure to the risk concerned.
12.	Diseases caused by manganese or its toxic compounds.	All work involving exposure to the risk concerned.
13.	Skin diseases caused by physical, chemical or biological agents not included in other items.	All work involving exposure to the risk concerned.
14.	Hearing impairment caused by noise.	All work involving exposure to the risk concerned.
15.	Poisoning by dinitrophenol or a homologue or by substituted dinitrophenol or by the salts of such substances.	All work involving exposure to the risk concerned.

16.	Diseases caused by beryllium of its toxic compounds.	All work involving exposure to the risk concerned.
17.	Diseases caused by cadmium or its toxic compounds	All work involving exposure to the risk concerned.
18.	Occupational asthma caused by recognised sensitising agents inherent to the work process.	All work involving exposure to the risk concerned.
19.	Diseases caused by fluorine or its toxic compounds.	All work involving exposure to the risk concerned.
20.	Diseases caused by nitroglycerine or other nitroacid esters.	All work involving exposure to the risk concerned.
21.	Diseases caused by alcohols and ketones.	All work involving exposure to the risk concerned.
22.	Diseases caused by asphyxiants:carbon monoxide, and its toxic derivatives, hydrogen sulfide.	All work involving exposure to the risk concerned.
23.	Lung cancer and mesothe liomas caused by asbestos.	All work involving exposure to the risk concerned.
24.	Primary neoplasm of the epithelial lining of the urinary bladder or the kidney or the ureter.	All work involving exposure to the risk concerned.
25.	Snow blindness in snow bound areas.	All work involving exposure to the risk concerned.
26.	Disease due to effect of heat in extreme hot climate.	All work involving exposure to the risk concerned.
27.	Disease due to effect of cold in extreme cold climate:	All work involving exposure to the risk concerned.]

PART C

1.	Pneumoconioses caused by sclerogenic mineral dust (silicosis, anthraoosilicosis, asbestosis) and silico-tuberculosis provided that silicosis is an essential factor in causing	All work involving exposure to the risk concerned.

the resultant incapacity or death.

2.	Bagassosis.	All work involving exposure to the risk concerned.
3.	Bronchopulmonary diseases caused by cotton, flax hemp and sisal dust (Byssinosis).	All work involving exposure to the risk concerned.
4.	Extrinsic allergic alveelitis caused by the inhalation of organic dusts.	All work involving exposure to the risk concerned.
5.	Bronchopulmonary diseases caused by hard metals.	All work involving exposure to the risk concerned.
6.	Acute Pulmonary Oedema of High Altitude.	All work involving exposure to the risk concerned.

SCHEDULE IV

(See section 4)

FACTORS FOR WORKING OUT LUMP SUM EQUIVALENT OF COMPENSATION AMOUNT IN CASE OF PERMANENT DISABLEMENT AND DEATH

Completed years of age on the last birthday of the the employee immediately preceding the date on which the compensation fell due	*Factors*
1	*2*
not more than 16	228.54
17	227.49
18	226.38
19	225.22
20	224.00
21	222.71
22	221.37
23	219.95
24	218.47
25	216.91
26	215.28
27	213.57
28	211.79
29	209.92
30	207.98
31	205.95
32	203.85
33	201.66
34	199.40
35	197.06

36	194.64
37	192.14
38	189.56
39	186.90
40	184.17
41	181.37
42	178.49
43	175.54
44	172.52
45	169.44
46	166.29
47	163.07
48	159.80
49	156.47
50	153.09
51	149.67
52	146.20
53	142.68
54	139.13
55	135.96
56	131.95
57	128.33
58	124.70
59	121.05
60	117.41
61	113.77
62	110.14
63	106.52
64	102.93
65 or more	99.37]

PAYMENT OF WAGES ACT, 1936
[Act No. 4 of Year 1936]

An Act to regulate the payment of wages of certain classes of [1][EMPLOYED PERSONS]
Whereas it is expedient to regulate the payment of wages to certain classes of [1][employed persons];
It is hereby enacted as follows: -

1. Short title, extent, commencement and application

(1) This Act may be called the Payment of Wages Act, 1936.

[2][(2) It extends to the whole of India [3][* * *]].

(3) It shall come into force on such [4][date] as the Central Government may, by notification in the Official Gazette, appoint.

(4) It applies in the first instance to the payment of wages to persons employed in any [5][factory, to persons] employed (otherwise than in a factory) upon any railway by a railway administration or, either directly or through a sub-contractor, by a person fulfilling a contract with a railway administration, [6][and to persons employed in an industrial or other establishment specified in sub-clauses (a) to (g) of clause (ii) of section 2.]

(5) The State Government may, after giving three months' notice of its intention of so doing, by notification in the Official Gazette, extend the provisions of [7][this Act] or any of them to the payment of wages to any class of persons employed in [8][any establishment or class of establishments specified by the Central Government or a State Government under sub-clause (h) of clause (ii) of section 2]:

[9][PROVIDED that in relation to any such establishment owned by the Central Government no such notification shall be issued except with the concurrence of that governments.]

(6) Nothing in this Act shall apply to wages payable in respect of a wage-period which, over such wage-period, average [10][one thousand six hundred rupees] a month or more.

2. Definitions

In this Act, unless there is anything repugnant in the subject or context,-

¹¹[(i) "employed person" includes the legal representative of a deceased employed person;

(ia) "employer" includes the legal representative of a deceased employer;

(ib) "factory" means a factory as defined in clause (m) of section 2 of the Factories Act, 1948 (63 of 1948) and includes any place to which the provisions of that Act have been applied under sub-section (1) of section 85 thereof;]

(ii) ¹²["industrial or other establishment"] means any-

¹¹[(a) tramway service, or motor transport service engaged in carrying passengers or goods or both by road for hire or reward;

(aa) air transport service other than such service belonging to, or exclusively employed in the military, naval or air forces of the Union or the Civil Aviation Department of the Government of India;]

(b) dock, wharf or jetty;

¹³[(c) inland vessel, mechanically propelled;]

(d) mine, quarry or oil-field;

(e) plantation;

(f) workshop or other establishment in which articles are produced, adapted or manufactured, with a view to their use, transport or sale;

¹⁴[(g) establishment in which any work relating to the construction, development or maintenance of buildings, roads, bridges or canals, or relating to operations connected with navigation, irrigation, or to the supply of water or relating to the generation, transmission and distribution of electricity or any other form of power is being carried on;]

⁶[(h) any other establishment or class of establishments which the Central Government or a State Government may, having regard to the nature thereof, the need for protection of persons employed therein and other relevant circumstances, specify, by notification in the Official Gazette.]

¹⁵[(iia) "mine" has the meaning assigned to it in clause (j) of sub-section (1) of section 2 of the Mines Act, 1952 (35 of 1952);]

¹¹[(iii) "plantation" has the meaning assigned to it in clause (f) of section 2 of the Plantations Labour Act, 1951 (69 of 1951);]

(iv) "prescribed" means prescribed by rules made under this Act;

(v) "railway administration" has the meaning assigned to it in clause (6) of section 3 of the Indian Railways Act, 1890 (9 of 1890); and

[13][(vi) "wages" means all remuneration (whether by way of salary, allowances, or otherwise) expressed in terms of money or capable of being so expressed which would, if the terms of employment, express or implied, were fulfilled, be payable to a person employed in respect of his employment or of work done in such employment, and includes-

(a) any remuneration payable under any award or settlement between the parties or order of a court;

(b) any remuneration to which the person employed is entitled in respect of overtime work or holidays or any leave period;

(c) any additional remuneration payable under the terms of employment (whether called a bonus or by any other name);

(d) any sum which by reason of the termination of employment of the person employed is payable under any law, contract or instrument which provides for the payment of such sum, whether with or without deductions, but does not provide for the time within which the payment is to be made;

(e) any sum to which the person employed is entitled under any scheme framed under any law for the time being in force,

but does not include-

(1) any bonus (whether under a scheme of profit sharing or otherwise) which does not form part of the remuneration payable under the terms of employment or which is not payable under any award or settlement between the parties or order of a court;

(2) the value of any house-accommodation, or of the supply of light, water, medical attendance or other amenity or of any service excluded from the computation of wages by a general or special order of the State Government;

(3) any contribution paid by the employer to any pension or provident fund, and the interest which may have accrued thereon;

(4) any travelling allowance or the value of any travelling concession;

(5) any sum paid to the employed person to defray special expenses entailed on him by the nature of his employment; or

(6) any gratuity payable on the termination of employment in cases other than those specified in sub-clause (d).]

3. Responsibility for payment of wages

Every employer shall be responsible for the payment to persons employed by him of all wages required to be paid under this Act:

PROVIDED that, in the case of persons employed (otherwise than by a contractor)-

(a) in factories, if a person has been named as the manager of the factory under [16][clause (f) of sub-section (1) of section 7 of the Factories Act, 1948 (63 of 1948)];

[17][(b) in industrial or other establishments, if there is a person responsible to the employer for the supervision and control of the industrial or other establishments;]

(c) upon railways (otherwise than in factories), if the employer is the railway administration and the railway administration has nominated a person in this behalf for the local area concerned.

The person so named, the person so responsible to the employer, or the person so nominated, as the case may be [18][shall also be responsible] for such payment.

4. Fixation of wage-periods

(1) Every person responsible for the payment of wages under section 3 shall fix periods (in this Act referred to as wage-periods) in respect of which such wages shall be payable.

(2) No wage-period shall exceed one month.

5. Time of payment of wages

(1) The wages of every person employed upon or in-

(a) any railway, factory or [12][industrial or other establishment] upon or in which less than one thousand persons are employed, shall be paid before the expiry of the seventh day,

(b) any other railway, factory or [12][industrial or other establishment], shall be paid before the expiry of the tenth day,

after the last day of the wage-period in respect of which the wages are payable:

[15][PROVIDED that in the case of persons employed on a dock, wharf or jetty or in a mine, the balance of wages found due on completion of the final tonnage account of the ship or wagons loaded or unloaded, as the case may be, shall be paid before the expiry of the seventh day from the day of such completion.]

(2) Where the employment of any person is terminated by or on behalf of the employer, the wages, earned by him shall be paid before the expiry of the second working day from the day on which his employment is terminated:

[15][PROVIDED that where the employment of any person in an establishment is terminated due to the closure of the establishment for any reason other than a weekly or other recognised holiday, the wages earned by him shall be paid before the expiry of the second day from the day on which his employment is so terminated]

(3) The State Government may, by general or special order, exempt, to such extent and subject to such conditions as may be specified in the order, the person responsible for the payment of wages to persons employed upon any railway (otherwise than in a factory) [15][or

to persons employed as daily-rated workers in the Public Works Department of the Central Government or the State Government] from the operation of this section in respect of wages of any such persons or class of such persons:

[15][PROVIDED that in the case of persons employed as daily-rated workers as aforesaid, no such order shall be made except in consultation with the Central Government.]

(4) [19][Save as otherwise provided in sub-section (2), all payments] of wages shall be made on a working day.

6. Wages to be paid in current coin or currency notes

All wages shall be paid in current coin or currency notes or in both:

[20][PROVIDED that the employer may, after obtaining the written authorisation of the employed person, pay him the wages either by cheque or by crediting the wages in his bank account.]

7. Deductions which may be made from wages

(1) Notwithstanding the provisions of sub-section (2) of section 47 of the Indian Railways Act, 1890 (9 of 1890), the wages of an employed person shall be paid to him without deductions of any kind except those authorised by or under this Act.

[21]*[Explanation I]* : Every payment made by the employed person to the employer or his agent shall, for the purposes of this Act, be deemed to be a deduction from wages.

[14]*[Explanation II:* Any loss of wages resulting from the imposition, for good and sufficient cause, upon a person employed of any of the following penalties, namely:-

(i) the withholding of increment or promotion (including the stoppage of increment at an efficiency bar);

(ii) the reduction to a lower post or time scale or to a lower stage in a time scale; or

(iii) suspension;

shall not be deemed to be a deduction from wages in any case where the rules framed by the employer for the imposition of any such penalty are in conformity with the requirements, if any, which may be specified in this behalf by the State Government by notification in the Official Gazette.]

(2) Deductions from the wages of an employed person shall be made only in accordance with the provisions of this Act, and may be of the following kinds only, namely:

(a) fines;

(b) deductions for absence from duty;

(c) deductions for damage to or loss of goods expressly entrusted to the employed person for custody, or for loss of money for which he is required to account, where such damage or loss is directly attributable to his neglect or default;

[13][(d) deductions for house-accommodation supplied by the employer or by government or any housing board set up under any law for the time being in force (whether the government or the board is the employer or not) or any other authority engaged in the business of subsidising house- accommodation which may be specified in this behalf by the State Government by notification in the Official Gazette;]

(e) deductions for such amenities and services supplied by the employer as the [22][***] State Government [15][or any officer specified by it in this behalf] may, by general or special order, authorise.

Explanation: The word "services" in [23][this clause] does not include the supply of tools and raw materials required for the purposes of employment;

[11][(f) deductions for recovery of advances of whatever nature (including advances for travelling allowance or conveyance allowance), and the interest due in respect thereof, or for adjustment of over-payments of wages;

(ff) deductions for recovery of loans made from any fund constituted for the welfare of labour in accordance with the rules approved by the State Government, and the interest due in respect thereof;

(fff) deductions for recovery of loans granted for house-building or other purposes approved by the State Government and the interest due in respect thereof;]

(g) deductions of income-tax payable by the employed person;

(h) deductions required to be made by order of a court or other authority competent to make such order;

(i) deductions for subscriptions to, and for repayment of advances from any provident fund to which the Provident Funds Act, 1925 (19 of 1925), applies or any recognised provident fund as defined in [24][section 58A of the Indian Income Tax Act, 1922 (11 of 1922)], or any provident fund approved in this behalf by the State Government, during the continuance of such approval; [25][***]

[26][(j) deductions for payments to co-operative societies approved by the State Government [15][or any officer specified by it in this behalf] or to a scheme of insurance maintained by the Indian Post Office, [27][and]

[13][(k) deductions, made with the written authorisation of the person employed for payment of any premium on his life insurance policy to the Life Insurance Corporation Act of India established under the Life Insurance Corporation Act, 1956 (31 of 1956), or for the purchase of securities of the Government of India or of any State Government or for being

deposited in any Post Office Savings Bank in furtherance of any savings scheme of any such government.]]

[6][(kk) deductions, made with the written authorisation of the employed person, for the payment of his contribution to any fund constituted by the employer or a trade union registered under the Trade Union Act, 1926 (16 of 1926), for the welfare of the employed persons or the members of their families, or both, and approved by the State Government or any officer specified by it in this behalf, during the continuance of such approval;

(kkk) deductions, made with the written authorisation of the employed person, for payment of the fees payable by him for the membership of any trade union registered under the Trade Union Act, 1926 (16 of 1926);]

[15][(l) deductions, for payment of insurance premia on Fidelity Guarantee Bonds;

(m) deductions for recovery of losses sustained by a railway administration on account of acceptance by the employed person of counterfeit or base coins or mutilated or forged currency notes;

(n) deductions for recovery of losses sustained by a railway administration on account of the failure of the employed person to invoice, to bill, to collect or to account for the appropriate charges due to that administration whether in respect of fares, freight, demurrage, wharfage and cranage or in respect of sale of food in catering establishments or in respect of sale of commodities in grain shops or otherwise;

(o) deductions for recovery of losses sustained by a railway administration on account of any rebates or refunds incorrectly granted by the employed person where such loss is directly attributable to his neglect or default;]

[20][(p) deductions, made with the written authorisation of the employed person, for contribution to the Prime Minister's National Relief Fund or to such other Fund as the Central Government may, by notification in the Official Gazette, specify;]

[28][(q) deductions for contributions to any insurance scheme framed by the Central Government for the benefit of its employees.]

[15][(3) Notwithstanding anything contained in this Act, the total amount of deductions which may be made under sub-section (2) in any wage-period from the wages of any employed person shall not exceed-

(i) in cases where such deductions are wholly or partly made for payments to co-operative societies under clause (j) of sub-section (2), seventy-five per cent of such wages, and

(ii) in any other case, fifty per cent of such wages:

PROVIDED that where the total deductions authorised under sub-section (2) exceed seventy five per cent or, as the case may be, fifty per cent of the wages, the excess may be recovered in such manner as may be prescribed.

(4) Nothing contained in this section shall be construed as precluding the employer from recovering from the wages of the employed person or otherwise any amount payable By such person under any law for the time being in force other than the Indian Railways Act, 1890 (9 of 1890).]

8. *Fines*

(1) No fine shall be imposed on any employed person save in respect of such acts and omissions on his part as the employer, with the previous approval of the State Government or of the prescribed authority, may have specified by notice under sub-section (2).

(2) A notice specifying such acts and omissions shall be exhibited in the prescribed manner on the premises in which the employment is carried on or in the case of persons employed upon a railway (otherwise than in a factory), at the prescribed place or places.

(3) No fine shall be imposed on any employed person until he has been given an opportunity of showing cause against the fine, or otherwise than in accordance with such procedure as may be prescribed for the imposition of fines.

(4) The total amount of fine which may be imposed in any one wage-period on any employed person shall not exceed an amount equal to [29][three per cent] of the wages payable to him in respect of that wage-period.

(5) No fine shall be imposed on any employed person who is under the age of fifteen years.

(6) No fine imposed on any employed person shall be recovered from him by instalments or after the expiry of sixty days from the day on which it was imposed.

(7) Every fine shall be deemed to have been imposed on the day of the act or omission in respect of which it was imposed.

(8) All fines and all realisations thereof shall be recorded in a register to be kept by the person responsible for the payment of wages under section 3 in such form as may be prescribed; and all such realisations shall be applied only to such purposes beneficial to the persons employed in the factory or establishment as are approved by the prescribed authority.

Explanation : When the persons employed upon or in any railway, factory or [12][industrial or other establishment] are part only of a staff employed under the same management, all such realisations may be credited to a common fund maintained for the staff as a whole, provided that the fund shall be applied only to such purposes as are approved by the prescribed authority.

9. Deductions for absence from duty

(1) Deductions may be made under clause (b) of sub-section (2) of section 7 only on account of the absence of an employed person from the place or places where, by the terms of his employment, he is required to work, such absence being for the whole or any part of the period during which he is so required to work.

(2) The amount of such deduction shall in no case bear to the wages payable to the employed person in respect of the wage-period for which the deduction is made in a larger proportion than the period for which he was absent bears to the total period, within such wage-period, during which by the terms of his employment, he was required to work:

PROVIDED that, subject to any rules made in this behalf by the State Government, if ten or more employed persons acting in concert absent themselves without due notice (that is to say without giving the notice which is required under the terms of their contracts of employment) and without reasonable cause, such deduction from any such person may include such amount not exceeding his wages for eight days as may by any such terms be due to the employer in lieu of due notice.

[30][*Explanation* : For the purposes of this section, an employed person shall be deemed to be absent from the place where he is required to work if, although present in such place, he refuses, in pursuance of a stay-in strike or for any other cause which is not reasonable in the circumstances, to carry out his work.]

10. Deductions for damage or loss

[11][(1) A deduction under clause (c) or clause (o) of sub-section (2) of section 7 shall not exceed the amount of the damage or loss caused to the employer by the neglect or default of the employed person.

(1A) A deduction shall not be made under clause (c) or clause (m) or clause (n) or clause (o) of sub-section (2) of section 7 until the employed person has been given an opportunity of showing cause against the deduction or otherwise than in accordance with such procedure as may be prescribed for the making of such deduction.]

(2) All such deduction and all realisations thereof shall be recorded in a register to be kept by the person responsible for the payment of wages under section 3 in such form as may be prescribed.

11. Deductions for services rendered

A deduction under clause (d) or clause (e) of sub-section (2) of section 7 shall not be made from the wages of an employed person, unless the house-accommodation amenity or service has been accepted by him, as a term of employment or otherwise, and such deduction shall not exceed an amount equivalent to the value of the house-accommodation amenity or service supplied and, in the case of deduction under the said clause (e), shall be subject to such conditions as [22][***] the State Government may impose.

12. Deductions for recovery of advances

Deductions under clause (f) of sub-section (2) of section 7 shall be subject to the following conditions, namely:

(a) recovery of an advance of money given before employment began shall be made from the first payment of wages in respect of a complete wage-period, but no recovery shall be made of such advances given for travelling-expenses;

[15][(aa) recovery of an advance of money given after employment began shall be subject to such conditions as the State Government may impose;]

(b) recovery of advances of wages not already earned shall be subject to any rules made by the State Government regulating the extent to which such advances may be given and the instalments by which they may be recovered.

[15][12A. Deductions for recovery of loans

Deductions for recovery of loans granted under clause (fff) of sub-section (2) of section 7 shall be subject to any rules made by the State Government regulating the extent to which such loans may be granted and the rate of interest payable thereon.]

13. Deductions for payments to co-operative societies and insurance schemes

Deductions under clause (j) [27][and clause (k)] of sub-section (2) of section 7 shall be subject to such conditions as the State Government may impose.

[15][13A. Maintenance of registers and records

(1) Every employer shall maintain such registers and records giving such particulars of persons employed by him, the work performed by them, the wages paid to them, the deductions made from their wages, the receipts given by them and such other particulars and in such form as may be prescribed.

(2) Every register and record required to be maintained under this section shall, for the purposes of this Act, be preserved for a period of three years after the date of the last entry made therein].

14. Inspectors

(1) An Inspector of Factories appointed under [31][sub-section (1) of section 8 of the Factories Act, 1948 (63 of 1948)], shall be an Inspector for the purposes of this Act in respect of all factories within the local limits assigned to him.

(2) The State Government may appoint Inspectors for the purposes of this Act in respect of all persons employed upon a railway (otherwise than in a factory) to whom this Act applies.

(3) The State Government may, by notification in the Official Gazette, appoint such other persons as it thinks fit to be Inspectors for the purposes of this Act, and may define the local limits within which and the class of factories and [12][industrial or other establishments] in respect of which they shall exercise their functions.

[11][(4) An Inspector may,

(a) make such examination and inquiry as he thinks fit in order to ascertain whether the provisions of this Act or rules made thereunder are being observed;

(b) with such assistance, if any, as he thinks fit, enter, inspect and search any premises of any railway, factory or [12][industrial or other establishment] at any reasonable time for the purpose of carrying out the objects of this Act;

(c) supervise the payment of wages to persons employed upon any railway or in any factory or [12][industrial or other establishment];

(d) require by a written order the production at such place, as may be prescribed, of any register maintained in pursuance of this Act and take on the spot or otherwise statements of any persons which he may consider necessary for carrying out the purposes of this Act;

(e) seize or take copies of such registers or documents or portions thereof as he may consider relevant in respect of an offence under this Act which he has reason to believe has been committed by an employer;

(f) exercise such other powers as may be prescribed:

PROVIDED that no person shall be compelled under this sub-section to answer any question or make any statement tending to incriminate himself.]

(4A) The provisions of the [32][Code of Criminal Procedure, 1973 (2 of 1974)]shall, so far as may be, apply to any search or seizure under this sub-section as they apply to any search or seizure made under the authority of a warrant issued under [33][section 94] of the said Code].

(5) Every Inspector shall be deemed to be a public servant within the meaning of the Indian Penal Code, 1860 (45 of 1860).

[15][14A. Facilities to be afforded to Inspectors

Every employer shall afford an Inspector all reasonable facilities for making any entry, inspection, supervision, examination or inquiry under this Act.]

15. Claims arising out of deductions from wages or delay in payment of wages and penalty for malicious or vexatious claims

(1) The State Government may, by notification in the Official Gazette, appoint [15][a presiding officer of any Labour Court or Industrial Tribunal, constituted under the Industrial Disputes Act, 1947 (14 of 1947), or under any corresponding law relating to the investigation and settlement of industrial disputes in force in the State or] any Commissioner for Workmen's Compensation or other officer with experience as a Judge of a Civil Court or as a Stipendiary Magistrate to be the authority to hear and decide for any specified area all claims arising out of deductions from the wages, or delay in payment of the wages, [34][of persons employed or paid in that area, including all matters, incidental to such claims:

PROVIDED that where the State Government considers it necessary so to do, it may appoint more than one authority for any specified area and may, by general or special order, provide for the distribution or allocation of work to be performed by them under this Act.]

(2) Where contrary to the provisions of this Act any deduction has been made from the wages of an employed person, or any payment of wages has been delayed, such person himself, or any legal practitioner or any official of a registered trade union authorised in writing to act on his behalf, or any Inspector under this Act, or any other person acting with the permission of the authority appointed under sub-section (1), may apply to such authority for a direction under sub-section (3):

PROVIDED that every such application shall be presented within [35][twelve months] from the date on which the deduction from the wages was made or from the date on which the payment of the wages was due to be made, as the case may be:

PROVIDED FURTHER that any application may be admitted after the said period [35][twelve months] when the applicant satisfies the authority that he had sufficient cause for not making the application within such period.

(3) When any application under sub-section (2) is entertained, the authority shall hear the applicant and the employer or other person responsible for the payment of wages under section 3, or give them an opportunity of being heard, and, after such
further inquiry (if any) as may be necessary, may, without prejudice to any other penalty to which such employer or other person is liable under this Act, direct the refund to the employed person of the amount deducted, or the payment of the delayed wages, together

with the payment of such compensation as the authority may think fit, not exceeding ten times the amount deducted in the former case and [36][not exceeding twenty-five rupees in the latter, and even if the amount deducted or the delayed wages are paid before the disposal of the application, direct the payment of such compensation, as the authority may think fit, not exceeding twenty-five rupees]:

PROVIDED that no direction for the payment of compensation shall be made in the case of delayed wages if the authority is satisfied that the delay was due to-

(a) a bona fide error or bona fide dispute as to the amount payable to the employed person, or

(b) the occurrence of an emergency, or the existence of exceptional circumstances, such that the person responsible for the payment of the wages was unable, though exercising reasonable diligence, to make prompt payment, or

(c) the failure of the employed person to apply for or accept payment.

[11][(4) If the authority hearing an application under this section is satisfied-

(a) that the application was either malicious or vexatious, the authority may direct that a penalty not exceeding fifty rupees be paid to the employer or other person responsible for the payment of wages by the person presenting the application; or

(b) that in any case in which compensation is directed to be paid under sub-section (3), the applicant ought not to have been compelled to seek redress under this section, the authority may direct that a penalty not exceeding fifty rupees be paid to the State Government by the employer or other person responsible for the payment of wages.

(4A) Where there is any dispute as to the person or persons being the legal representative or representatives of the employer or of the employed person, the decision of the authority on such dispute shall be final.

(4B) Any inquiry under this section shall be deemed to be a judicial proceeding within the meaning of sections 193, 219 and 228 of the Indian Penal Code (45 of 1860).]

(5) Any amount directed to be paid under this section may be recovered-

(a) if the authority is a Magistrate, by the authority as if it were a fine imposed by him as Magistrate, and

(b) if the authority is not a Magistrate, by any Magistrate to whom the authority makes application in this behalf, as if it were a fine imposed by such Magistrate.

16. Single application in respect of claims from unpaid group

(1) Employed persons are said to belong to the same unpaid group if they are borne on the same establishment and if [15][deductions have been made from their wages in contravention of this Act for the same cause and during the same wage-period or periods or

if] their wages for the same wage-period or periods have remained unpaid after the day fixed by section 5.

(2) A single application may be presented under section 15 on behalf or in respect of any number of employed persons belonging to the same unpaid group, and in such case [11][every person on whose behalf such application is presented may be awarded maximum compensation to the extent specified in sub-section (3) of section 15].

(3) The authority may deal with any number of separate pending applications, presented under section 15 in respect of persons belonging to the same unpaid group, as a single application presented under sub-section (2) of this section, and the provisions of that sub-section shall apply accordingly.

17. *Appeal*

(1) [37][An appeal against an order dismissing either wholly or in part an application made under sub-section (2) of section 15, or against a direction made under sub-section (3) or sub-section (4) of that section] may be preferred, within thirty days of the date on which [38][the order or direction] was made, in a Presidency-town [39][***] before the Court of Small Causes and elsewhere before the District Court-

(a) by the employer or other person responsible for the payment of wages under section 3, if the total sum directed to be paid by way of wages and compensation exceeds three hundred rupees [15][or such direction has the effect of imposing on the employer or the other person a financial liability exceeding one thousand rupees], or

[11][(b) by an employed person or any legal practitioner or any official of a registered trade union authorised in writing to act on his behalf or any Inspector under this Act, or any other person permitted by the authority to make an application under sub-section (2) of section 15, if the total amount of wages claimed to have been withheld from the employed person exceeds twenty rupees or from the unpaid group to which the employed person belongs or belonged exceeds fifty rupees, or]

(c) by any person directed to pay a penalty under sub-section (4) of section 15.

[15][(1A) No appeal under clause (a) of sub-section (1) shall lie unless the memorandum of appeal is accompanied by a certificate by the authority to the effect that the appellant has deposited the amount payable under the direction appealed against.]

[13][(2) Save as provided in sub-section (1) any order dismissing either wholly or in part an application made under sub-section (2) of section 15, or a direction made under sub-section (3) or sub-section (4) of that section shall be final.]

[65][(3) Where an employer prefers an appeal under this section the authority against whose decision the appeal has been preferred may, and if so directed by the court referred to in

sub-section (1) shall, pending the decision of the appeal, withhold payment of any sum in deposit with it.

(4) The court referred to in sub-section (1) may if it thinks fit submit any question of law for the decision of the High Court and, if it so does, shall decide the question in conformity with such decision.]

[14][17A. Conditional attachment of property of employer or other person responsible for payment of wages

(1) Where at any time after an application has been made under sub-section (2) of section 15 the authority, or where at any time after an appeal has been filed under section 17 by an employed person or [11][any legal practitioner or any official of a registered trade union authorised in writing to act on his behalf or any Inspector under this Act or any other person permitted by the authority to make an application under sub-section (2) of section 15] the Court referred to in that section, is satisfied that the employer or other person responsible for the payment of wages under section 3 is likely to evade payment of any amount that may be directed to be paid under section 15 or section 17, the authority or the court, as the case may be, except in cases where the authority or court is of the opinion that the ends of justice would be defeated by the delay, after giving the employer or other person an opportunity of being heard, may direct the attachment of so much of the property of the employer or other person responsible for the payment of wages as is, in the opinion of the authority or court, sufficient to satisfy the amount which may be payable under the direction.

(2) The provisions of the Code of Civil Procedure, 1908 (5 of 1908), relating to attachment before judgement under that Code shall, so far as may be, apply to any order for attachment under sub-section (1).]

18. Powers of authorities appointed under section 15

Every authority appointed under sub-section (1) of section 15 shall have all the powers of a civil court under the Code of Civil Procedure, 1908 (5 of 1908), for the purpose of taking evidence and of enforcing the attendance of witnesses and compelling the production of documents, and every such authority shall be deemed to be a civil court for all the purposes of section 195 and of [40][Chapter XXVI of the Code of Criminal Procedure, 1973 (2 of 1974).]

19. Power to recover from employer in certain cases [Repealed by the Payment of Wages (Amendment) Act, 1964 (53 of 1964), w.e.f. 1st. February, 1965]

20. Penalty for offences under the Act

(1) Whoever being responsible for the payment of wages to an employed person contravenes any of the provisions of any of the following sections, namely, [41][section 5 except sub-section (4) thereof, section 7, section 8 except sub-section (8) thereof, section 9, section 10 except sub-section (2) thereof, and section 11 to 13], both inclusive, shall be punishable with fine [42][which shall not be less than two hundred rupees but which may extend to one thousand rupees.]

(2) Whoever contravenes the provisions of section 4, [43][sub-section (4) of section 5, section 6, sub-section (8) of section 8, sub-section (2) of section 10] or section 25 shall be punishable with fine which may extend to [44][five hundred rupees.]

[15][(3) Whoever being required under this Act to maintain any records or registers or to furnish any information or return-

(a) fails to maintain such register or record; or

(b) wilfully refuses or without lawful excuse neglects to furnish such information or return; or

(c) wilfully furnishes or causes to be furnished any information or return which he knows to be false; or

(d) refuses to answer or wilfully gives a false answer to any question necessary for obtaining any information required to be furnished under this Act,

shall, for each such offence, be punishable with fine [45][which shall not be less than two hundred rupees but which may extend to one thousand rupees].

(4) Whoever-

(a) wilfully obstructs an Inspector in the discharge of his duties under this Act; or

(b) refuses or wilfully neglects to afford an Inspector any reasonable facility for making any entry, inspection, examination, supervision, or inquiry authorised by or under this Act in relation to any railway, factory or [12][industrial or other establishment]; or

(c) wilfully refuses to produce on the demand of an Inspector any register or other document kept in pursuance of this Act; or

(d) prevents or attempts to prevent or does anything which he has any reason to believe is likely to prevent any person from appearing before or being examined by an Inspector acting in pursuance of his duties under this Act;

shall be punishable with fine [45][which shall not be less than two hundred rupees but which may extend to one thousand rupees.]

(5) If any person who has been convicted of any offence punishable under this Act is again guilty of an offence involving contravention of the same provision, he shall be punishable on a subsequent conviction with imprisonment for a term [46][which shall not be

less than one month but which may extend to six months and with fine which shall not be less than five hundred rupees but which may extend to three thousand rupees]:

PROVIDED that for the purpose of this sub-section no cognizance shall be taken of any conviction made more than two years before the date on which the commission of the offence which is being punished came to the knowledge of the Inspector.

(6) If any person fails or wilfully neglects to pay the wages of any employed person by the date fixed by the authority in this behalf, he shall, without prejudice to any other action that may be taken against him, be punishable with an additional fine which may extend to [47][one hundred rupees] for each day for which such failure or neglect continues.]

21. Procedure in trial of offences

(1) No court shall take cognizance of a complaint against any person for an offence under sub-section (1) of section 20 unless an application in respect of the facts constituting the offence has been presented under section 15 and has been granted wholly or in part and the authority empowered under the latter section or the appellate Court granting such application has sanctioned the making of the complaint.

(2) Before sanctioning the making of a complaint against any person for an offence under sub-section (1) of section 20, the authority empowered under section 15 or the appellate Court, as the case may be, shall give such person an opportunity of showing cause against the granting of such sanction, and the sanction shall not be granted if such person satisfies the authority or Court that his default was due to-

(a) a bona fide error or bona fide dispute as to the amount payable to the employed person, or

(b) the occurrence of an emergency or the existence of exceptional circumstances, such that the person responsible for the payment of the wages was unable, though exercising reasonable diligence, to make prompt payment, or

(c) the failure of the employed person to apply for or accept payment.

(3) No Court shall take cognizance of a contravention of section 4 or of section 6 or of a contravention of any rule made under section 26 except on a complaint made by or with the sanction of an Inspector under this Act.

[15][(3A) No Court shall take cognizance of any offence punishable under sub-section (3) or sub-section (4) of section 20 except on a complaint made by or with the sanction of an Inspector under this Act.]

(4) In imposing any fine for an offence under sub-section (1) of section 20 the court shall take into consideration the amount of any compensation already awarded against the accused in any proceedings taken under section 15.

22. Bar of suits

No Court shall entertain any suit for the recovery of wages or of any deduction from wages in so far as the sum so claimed-

(a) forms the subject of an application under section 15 which has been presented by the plaintiff and which is pending before the authority appointed under that section or of an appeal under section 17; or

(b) has formed the subject of a direction under section 15 in favour of the plaintiff; or

(c) has been adjudged, in any proceeding under section 15, not to be owed to the plaintiff; or

(d) could have been recovered by an application under section 15.

[15][22A. Protection of action taken in good faith

No suit, prosecution or other legal proceeding shall lie against the government or any officer of the government for anything which is in good faith done or intended to be done under this Act.]

23. Contracting out

Any contract or agreement, whether made before or after the commencement of this Act, whereby an employed person relinquishes any right conferred by this Act shall be null and void in so far as it purports to deprive him of such right.

[48][24. Application of Act to railways, air transport services, mines and oilfields

The powers by this act conferred upon the State Government shall, in relation to [49][railways], [15][air transport services,] mines and oilfields, be powers of the Central Government.]

25. Display by notice of abstracts of the Act

The person responsible for the payment of wages to persons ; [50][employed in a factory or an industrial or other establishment] shall cause to be [51][displayed in such factory or industrial or other establishment] a notice containing such abstracts of this Act and of the rules made thereunder in English and in the language of the majority of the persons employed [52][in the factory, or industrial or other establishment], as may be prescribed.

[53][25A. Payment of undisbursed wages in case of death of employed person

(1) Subject to the other provisions of the Act all amounts payable to an employed person as wages shall, if such amounts could not or cannot be paid on account of his death before payment or on account of his whereabouts not being known,-

(a) be paid to the person nominated by him in this behalf in accordance with the rules made under this Act; or

(b) where no such nomination has been made or where for any reasons such amounts cannot be paid to the person so nominated, be deposited with the prescribed authority who shall deal with the amounts so deposited in such manner as may be prescribed.

(2) Where, in accordance with the provisions of sub-section (1), all amounts payable to an employed person as wages-

(a) are paid by the employer to the person nominated by the employed person; or

(b) are deposited by the employer with the prescribed authority,

the employer shall be discharged of his liability to pay those wages.]

26. Rule-making power

(1) The State Government may make rules to regulate the procedure to be followed by the authorities and courts referred to in sections 15 and 17.

(2) The State Government may, [89][***] by notification in the Official Gazette, make rules for the purpose of carrying into effect the provisions of this Act.

(3) In particular and without prejudice to the generality of the foregoing power, rules made under sub-section (2) may-

(a) require the maintenance of such records, registers, returns and notices as are necessary for the enforcement of the Act [54][prescribe the form thereof and the particulars to be entered in such registers or records];

(b) require the display in a conspicuous place on premises where employment is carried on of notices specifying rates of wages payable to persons employed on such premises;

(c) Provide for the regular inspection of the weights, measures and weighing machines used by employers in checking or ascertaining the wages of persons employed by them;

(d) prescribe the manner of giving notice of the days on which wages will be paid;

(e) prescribe the authority competent to approve under sub-section (1) of section 8 acts and omissions in respect of which fines may be imposed;

(f) prescribe the procedure for the imposition of fines under section 8 and for the making of the deductions referred to in section 10;

(g) prescribe the conditions subject to which deductions may be made under the proviso to sub-section (2) of section 9;

(h) prescribe the authority competent to approve the purposes on which the proceeds of fines shall be expended;

(i) prescribe the extent to which advances may be made and the instalments by which they may be recovered with reference to clause (b) of section 12;

15[(ia) prescribe the extent to which loans may be granted and the rate of interest payable thereon with reference to section 12A,.

(ib) prescribe the powers of Inspectors for the purposes of this Act;]

(j) regulate the scale of costs which may allowed in proceedings under this Act;

(k) prescribe the amount of court-fees payable in respect of any proceedings under this Act, 55[***]

(l) prescribe the abstracts to be contained in the notices required by section 25; 56[***]

6[(la) prescribe the form and manner in which nominations may be made for the purposes of sub-section (1) of section 25A, the cancellation or variation of any such nomination, or the making of any fresh nomination in the event of the nominee predeceasing the person making nomination, and other matters connected with such nominations;

(lb) specify the authority with whom amounts required to be deposited under clause (b) of sub-section (1) of section 25A shall be deposited, and the manner in which such authority shall deal with the amounts deposited with it under that clause;]

6[(m) provide for any other matter which is to be or may be prescribed.]

(4) In making any rule under this section the State Government may provide that a contravention of the rule shall be punishable with fine which may extend to two hundred rupees.

(5) All rules made under this section shall be subject to the condition of previous publication, and the date to be specified under clause (3) of section 23 of the General Clauses Act, 1897 (10 of 1897), shall not be less than three months from the date on which the draft of the proposed rules was published.

6[(6) Every rule made by the Central Government under this section shall be laid, as soon as may be after it is made, before each House of Parliament while it is in session for a total period of thirty days which may be comprised in one session or in 57[two or more successive sessions,] and if, before the expiry of the session 58[immediately following the session or the successive sessions aforesaid,] both Houses agree in making any modification in the rule, or both Houses agree that the rule should not be made, the rule shall thereafter have effect only in such modified form or be of no effect, as the case may be; so however, that any such modification or annulment shall be without prejudice to the validity of anything previously done under that rule.]

Foot Notes

1 Substituted by Act No. 38 of 1982, for the words "persons employed in industry" w.e.f. 15th. October, 1982.

2 Substituted for sub-section (2) by the Adaptation of Laws Order, 1950.

3 Omitted by Act No. 51 of 1970, w.e.f. 1st. September, 1971.

4 28-3-1937, see Gazette of India, 1937, Part I, page 626.

5 Substituted by Act No. 38 of 1982, for the words "factory and to persons" w.e.f. 15th. October, 1982.

6 Inserted by Act No. 38 of 1982, w.e.f. 15th. October, 1982.

7 Substituted by Act No. 68 of 1957, for the words "the Act" w.e.f. 1st. April, 1958.

8 Substituted for the words "any industrial establishment or in any class or group of industrial establishments" by Act No. 38 of 1982, w.e.f. 15th. October, 1982.

9 Substituted by Act No. 38 of 1982, for the proviso w.e.f. 15th. October, 1982.

10 Substituted by Act No. 38 of 1982, for the words "one thousand rupees" , w.e.f. 15th. October, 1982.

11 Substituted by Act No. 53 of 1964, w.e.f. 1st. February, 1965.

12 Substituted by Act No. 38 of 1982, for the words "industrial establishment", w.e.f. 15th. October, 1982.

13 Substituted by Act No. 68 of 1957, w.e.f. 1st. April, 1958.

14 Inserted by Act No. 68 of 1957, w.e.f. 1st. April, 1958.

15 Inserted by Act No. 53 of 1964, w.e.f. 1st. February, 1965.

16 Substituted by Act No. 68 of 1957, for the words, brackets and figures "clause (e) of sub-section (1) of section 9 of Factories Act, 1934", w.e.f. 1st. April, 1958.

17 Substituted by Act No. 38 of 1982, w.e.f. 15th. October, 1982.

18 Substituted by Act No. 53 of 1964, for the words "shall be responsible" w.e.f. 1st. February, 1965.

19 Substituted by Act No. 53 of 1964 for the words "All payments" w.e.f. 1st. February, 1965.

20 Inserted by Act No. 29 of 1976, w.e.f. 12-11-1975.

21 Explanation re-numbered as Explanation 1 by Act No. 68 of 1957, w.e.f. 1st. April, 1958.

22 The words "Governor- General in Council or" omitted by Govt. of India (Adap. of Indian Laws) Order, 1937.

23 Substituted by Act No. 56 of 1974, Sch. II, for the words "this sub-clause".

24 Refer to corresponding provision of Income Tax Act, 1961.

25 The word "and" omitted by Ordinance 3 of 1940.

26 When the Defence of India Act, 1971 is in existence, section 7 of the Act would have full effect as if after clause (i) the following clause (ii) stood in force:

"(ii) deductions made with the written authorisation of-

(i) The employed person; or

(ii) the president or secretary of the registered trade union of which the employed person is a member on such conditions as may be prescribed, for contribution to the National Defence Fund or to any Defence Savings Scheme approved by the State Government;".

27 Inserted by Ordinance 3 of 1940.

28 Inserted by Act No. 19 of 1977

29 Substituted by Act No. 38 of 1982, for the words "half -an-anna in the rupee", w.e.f. 15th. October, 1982.

30 Added by Act No. 22 of 1937.

31 Substituted by Act No. 68 of 1957, for the words, brackets and figures "sub-section (1) of section 10 of the Factories Act, 1934" w.e.f. 1st. April, 1958.

32 Substituted by Act No. 38 of 1982, for the figures "Cr. P. C., 1898", w.e.f. 15th. October, 1982.

33 Substituted by Act No. 38 of 1982, for the words "section 98" w.e.f. 15th. October, 1982.

34 Substituted by Act No. 53 of 1964 for the words "of persons employed or paid in that area" w.e.f. 1st. February, 1965.

35 Substituted by Act No. 53 of 1964, for the words "six months" w.e.f. 1st. February, 1965.

36 Substituted by Act No. 53 of 1964, for the words "not exceeding ten rupees in the latter", w.e.f. 1st. February, 1965.

37 Substituted by Act No. 68 of 1957, for the words, brackets and figures "An appeal against a direction made under sub-section (3) or sub-section (4) of section 15" w.e.f. 1st. April, 1958.

38 Substituted by Act No. 68 of 1957 for the words "the direction", w.e.f. 1st. April, 1958.

39 The words "or in Rangoon" omitted by the Government of India (Adaptation of Indian Laws) Order, 1937.

40 Substituted for "Chapter XXXV of the Code of Criminal Procedure, 1898" by Act No. 38 of 1982, w.e.f. 15th. October, 1982.

41 Substituted by Act No. 53 of 1964, for the words and figures "section 5 and sections 7 to 13" w.e.f. 1st. February, 1965.

42 Substituted by Act No. 38 of 1982, for the words "which may extend to five hundred rupees" w.e.f. 15th. October, 1982.

43 Substituted by Act No. 53 of 1964, for the word and figure "section 6" w.e.f. 1st. February, 1965.

44 Substituted by Act No. 38 of 1982, for the words "two hundred rupees" w.e.f. 15th. October, 1982.

45 Substituted by Act No. 38 of 1982, for the words "which may extend to five hundred rupees" w.e.f. 15th. October, 1982.

46 Substituted by Act No. 38 of 1982, for the words "which may extend to three months or with fine which may extend to one thousand rupees or with both" w.e.f. 15th. October, 1982.

47 Substituted for the words "fifty rupees" by Act No. 38 of 1982, w.e.f. 15th. October, 1982.

48 Substituted by the Government of India (Adaptation of Indian Laws) Order, 1937, for the original section 24.

49 Substituted by the Adaptation of Laws Order, 1950, for the words, brackets and figures "Federal railways (within the meaning of the Government of India Act, 1935)".

50 Substituted by Act No. 38 of 1982, for the words "employed in a factory" w.e.f. 15th. October, 1982.

51 Substituted by Act No. 38 of 1982, for the words "displayed in such factory" w.e.f. 15th. October, 1982.

52 Substituted by Act No. 38 of 1982, for the words "in the factory" w.e.f. 15th. October, 1982.

53 Inserted by Act No. 38 of 1982, w.e.f. 1st. March, 1994 vide GSR 287 (E) dated 1st. March, 1994.

54 Substituted by Act No. 53 of 1964, for the words "and prescribe the form thereof" w.e.f. 1st. February, 1965.

55 The word "and" omitted by Act No. 53 of 1964, w.e.f. 1st. February, 1965.

56 The word "and" omitted by Act No. 38 of 1982 w.e.f. 15th. October, 1982.

57 Substituted by Act No. 38 of 1982, for the words "two successive sessions" w.e.f. 15th. October, 1982.

58 Substituted by Act No. 38 of 1982, for the words "in which it is so laid or session immediately following" w.e.f. 15th. October, 1982.

International Publication, peer reviewed by Lawbright.
http://lawbright.in/editorial-board.html

www.ingramcontent.com/pod-product-compliance
Lightning Source LLC
Chambersburg PA
CBHW071435180526
45170CB00001B/358